lonely

US & BRITISH VIRGIN ISLANDS

Mark Johanson, Joe Sills

Pick a white-sand beach based on the surf, shade or solitude. Hike through dense tropical forests, then cool off in colorful reefs. Step back in time at ancient petroglyph sites, colonial forts and the ruins of crumbling sugar plantations. Dine on a humble conch fritter, juicy ribs or the regal Anegada lobster. At the end of the day, toss back some painkillers (a local cocktail!) as you sway to the beat of a scratch band or steel-pan jamboree.

These are the US and British Virgin Islands.

TURN THE PAGE AND START PLANNING YOUR NEXT BEST TRIP →

The Settlement

Anegada 1G4

B R I T I S H   V I R G I N   I S L A N D S   (U K)

Necker Island

Prickly Pear Island

Mosquito Island

Leverick Bay

Virgin Gorda 1G6

Gorda Peak

Spanish Town

Fallen Jerusalem

Ginger Island

Cooper Island

The Dogs

Scrub Island

Salt Island

Peter Island

Great Camanoe Island

Guana Island

East End

Spanish Town 20 min

Beef 20 min

Sir Francis Drake Channel

Norman Island

Tortola 1B3

Road Town ✪

The Settlement *1¼ hr*

Stage

Great Mountain

West End

Frenchmans Cay

Coral Bay

25 min

Great Thatch

Little Jost Van Dyke

Jost Van Dyke 1B2

Great Harbour

Coral Bay

Bordeaux Mountain

Virgin Islands National Park

St John G4

Cruz Bay

15 min

Great St James Island

Little St James Island

Cruz Bay

Caribbean Sea

Buck Island

Christiansted

St Croix 1B8

Mt Eagle

Frederiksted

Atlantic Ocean

Great Tobago

Little Tobago

Little Hans-Lollik Island

Inner Brass Island

Outer Brass Island

Hans Lollik Island

Thatch Cay

Red Hook

Lovango Cay

St Thomas 4'2

Magens Bay

Charlotte Amalie ✪

Water Island

Hassel Island

Capella Islands

Christiansted *2 hr*

Dutchcap Cay

Salt Cay

Cockroach Island

Savana Island

Saba Island

Crown Mountain

U S   V I R G I N   I S L A N D S   (U S)

0
20 km

0
10 miles

Meet our writers

Mark Johanson
@markonthemap

Mark is a former Virgin Islands resident who now roams the world for a variety of global travel magazines and newspapers. He still dreams about his years living in a tree house at Maho Bay, on St John.

Joe Sills

Joe is a travel writer, photographer and filmmaker who seeks out inspiring stories of conservation and human perseverance around the globe.

Cruz Bay (p68), St John

4

Contents

Best Experiences 6
Calendar 16
Trip Builder 24
7 Things to Know About
the Virgin Islands 34
Read, Listen,
Watch & Follow................ 36

US Virgin Islands   38
Practicalities..................... 40

St Thomas   42
Trip Builder 44
Practicalities..................... 45
Stroll Around Historic
Charlotte Amalie 46
Sun, Sand & Sea:
Pick Your Beach 48
Escape to the
'Fourth' Virgin 52
Take a Hike on
the West End 56
One Night in Red Hook 60
Listings 62

St John   64
Trip Builder 66
Practicalities......................67
Fall for 'Love City' 68
Hikes in Virgin
Islands National Park....... 70
Hiking the Reef Bay Trail...76
Beach-Hop the
North Shore...................... 80
Hiking & Snorkeling
Near Coral Bay 82
A Private Island
Experience........................ 84
Listings 86

St Croix   88
Trip Builder 90
Practicalities......................91
Stroll Through History
in Christiansted............... 92
Soak Up the Flavors......... 94
Escape to Buck Island 98
The Easternmost
Point in the USA 102
Roam the Wild
North Shore.....................104
Swim in Wild
Ocean Pools....................106
Explore Historic
Frederiksted 108
Listings 112

British Virgin Islands   114
Practicalities................... 116

Tortola   118
Trip Builder 120
Practicalities.................... 121
Wander the Waterfront
in Road Town 122
Revel at the Regatta........124
Learn to Surf in
Josiah's Bay....................126
Explore Secluded
Bays & Coves 128
The Lost World of
Sage Mountain 132
Find Paradise on
the North Shore 134
Paddleboard a
Shark Nursery.................136
Listings 140

Sailing Trip Through
the Little Sisters   142

Virgin Gorda   146
Trip Builder 148
Practicalities...................149
Scramble Through
the Baths 150
Bushwack Over
Gorda Peak 152
Kayak to Prickly
Pear Island.....................154
Snorkel & Savor
Savannah Bay 158
Live the High Life
at Oil Nut Bay 160
Listings 162

Anegada   164
Trip Builder 166
Practicalities...................167
Hover Over
Horseshoe Reef..............168
Live It Up at
Lobster Fest!................... 172
Spy Flamingos Through
a Looking Glass 174
Investigate
Conch Island 178
Listings 180

Jost Van Dyke   182
Trip Builder 184
Practicalities...................185
Swim to the
Soggy Dollar 186
Trek to the
Bubbly Pool 188

DAVID POLAKOFF/SHUTTERSTOCK

Anegada (p164)

Gallivant Around
Great Harbour 190
Jost Van Dyke
Bar-Hopping 194
Listings 196

Practicalities   198
Arriving 200
Getting Around 202
Safe Travel 204
Money 205
Accommodations 206
Responsible
Travel 208
Essentials 210

ESSAYS
Jump Up for Carnival 54
A Brief History
of the USVI 78
The 'Founding Father'
Raised in Christiansted 96
How Virgin are
the Islands? 110
Rewriting Maritime
History 130
Gli Gli: A Journey
Through Time,
Sea & Memory 138
The Ecological
Reality of the BVI 170
The Uneasy Economics
of Paradise 176
A Song of Reefs
& Rogues 192

VISUAL GUIDES
Local Souvenirs 58
The Animals of
the Virgin Islands 74
Undersea Life 156

0 ▲
N 0
20 km
10 miles

*Atlantic
Ocean*

Magens Bay Beach

A USVI Icon

Magens Bay gets packed for good reason. It's the only beach in the Virgin Islands located in a deep horseshoe bay, encased by lush green vegetation on both ends. This family-friendly option has all the facilities you could want and more.

🚗 *15 min north of Charlotte Amalie*

▶ p49

*Grea
Tobag*

*Hans-Lollik
Island*

*Crown
Mountain*

Charlotte Amalie ✪ *St Thomas*

° **Red
Hook**

P U E R T O
R I C O (U S)

Culebra

*Water
Island*

● **Ceiba**

U S V I R G I N
I S L A N D S
(U S)

*Sonda de
Vieques*

Vieques

SPECTACULAR
SANDS

*Caribbean
Sea*

▬▬▬ Beaches are, no doubt, the main draw for visitors to the Virgin Islands. They vary widely in atmosphere and landscape, from sheltered bays with shallow waters to windswept stretches edged by wild vegetation. Some are lively and easily reached, while others require a hike or boat ride to find complete isolation. What's certain: there's no shortage of spectacular sands.

Frederiksted ○

White Bay
Party Time!
Claim your place on the crazy-white sands of this famed beach on Jost Van Dyke where the painkiller (a local cocktail; pictured below) was born. Favored by hard-partying yachters and day-trippers from St John or St Thomas, this is the beach to go to for a good time.

🚶 30 min from Great Harbour
▶ p186

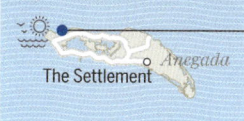

Cow Wreck Bay
Total Escape
Gone are the lush green hills of the other Virgins, which have volcanic origins. Anegada is instead a flat, sea-grape-covered isle formed by coral and limestone. Cow Wreck is its most appealing corner with two beach bars, a few kitesurfers and little else.

🚗 10 min north of The Settlement
▶ p169

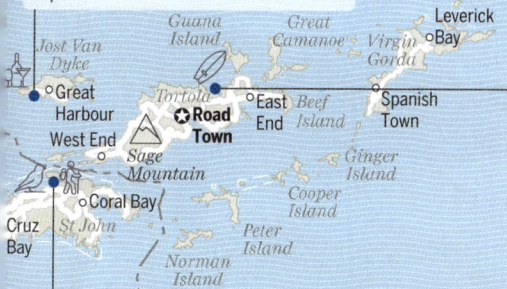

The Settlement · Anegada

BRITISH VIRGIN ISLANDS (UK)

Guana Island · Great Camanoe · Virgin Gorda · Leverick Bay · Spanish Town

Jost Van Dyke · Great Harbour · Tortola · Road Town · East End · Beef Island · Ginger Island

West End · Sage Mountain · Cooper Island

Coral Bay · St John · Peter Island

Cruz Bay · Norman Island

Josiah's Bay
Surf's Up
The normally calm Caribbean whips up enough swells along Tortola's northern coastline to make it attractive to surfers. Josiah's Bay, tucked beneath a rocky point, is the heart of the action and a great place to get atop a board for the first time.

🚗 15 min from Road Town
▶ p126

Francis Bay
Supreme Nature
The most secluded of the large bays in Virgin Islands National Park, Francis is the spot to escape from it all. You can hike into the woods just behind the beach to a bird-filled salt pond, or swim amid the seagrass searching for turtles.

🚗 25 min from Cruz Bay
▶ p73

Buck Island

St Croix · Christiansted

Jack and Isaac Bay Preserve
Turtle Time!
Tramp to a sequestered stretch of sandy coastline that's only accessible by foot. The Nature Conservancy manages these two neighboring beaches as part of a preserve for green and hawksbill turtles, which are active from July to December.

🚗 + 🚶 45 min east of Christiansted
▶ p102

UNLOCKING
HISTORY

The Virgin Islands were inhabited by various Amerindian groups before European powers planted their flags beginning in the 16th century. The Brits, Dutch, Danes, French and Spanish all built settlements here. Towering forts, crumbling sugar mills and the ruins of old plantation homes speak to this layered history.

KELLY VANDELLEN/SHUTTERSTOCK

→ TAÍNO PETROGLYPHS

Little remains from the Indigenous inhabitants of the Virgin Islands. You can, however, spot some faint Taíno petroglyphs just off the Reef Bay Trail, on St John.

Left Salt River Bay (p105) **Right** Petroglyphs, Reef Bay Trail (p76) **Below** Estate Whim Museum (p97)

← CHRISTOPHER COLUMBUS

Christopher Columbus made his first landing on what is now US soil at Salt River Bay National Historic Park on St Croix.

FROM LEFT: IMAGEBROKER.COM/ALAMY; IMAGEBROKER.COM/ALAMY

↑ THE LEGACY OF SLAVERY

Estate Whim Museum helps visitors contextualize 18th-century life in the Virgin Islands when it was run on a cruel system of slavery.

Best History Experiences

▶ **The Christiansted National Historic Site holds a large collection of Danish-colonial architecture.** (p93)

▶ **Grapple with the difficult history of slave-run planta-tions at the Annaberg Sugar Mill Ruins.** (p77)

▶ **The Danish-built Fort Chris-tian is the oldest standing structure in the USVI.** (p47)

▶ **Explore the continuation of an 800-year-old Arawak tradi-tion on Conch Island.** (p178)

▶ **Scuba dive to explore the RMS _Rhone_, a Royal Mail Steamer sunk in 1867.** (p145)

UNDER THE
SEA

If you thought the views above the water were good, then wait until you see what lies just under the surface. The Virgin Islands are ringed in prismatic coral reefs, making them a top-tier destination for snorkeling or diving. Most spots lie in shallow coves, and there are rarely strong currents, making it a great place for beginners to get their sea legs.

→ BOAT TRIPS

The best way to tackle several snorkel or dive spots is by boat. Every island has outfitters that can arrange group or custom trips.

▶ Sail through the Little Sisters (p142)

Left Leinster Bay (p82) **Right** Norman Island (p143) **Below** Diving near the Cane Bay Wall (p101)

SEAGRASS = SEA TURTLES

If your main goal is to spot sea turtles, you're better off skipping the reefs and going to beaches that are covered in seagrass.

▶ Discover the turtles of the Jack and Isaac Bay Preserve (p102)

↑ DEEP-SEA DIVES

Advanced divers will find no better scuba spot than the Cane Bay Wall, which plunges for thousands of feet just off St Croix's north shore.

Best Snorkel Experiences

▶ **Hike the Leinster Bay Trail, then swim to Waterlemon Cay for colorful corals and nurse sharks.** (p82)

▶ **Sail over from Christiansted to Buck Island to snorkel a rare elkhorn coral barrier reef.** (p98)

▶ **Explore the Indians, popular rock pinnacles that rise up from the water near Norman Island.** (p143)

▶ **Snorkel around boulders on uninhabited Prickly Pear Island looking for sea turtles and rays.** (p154)

VIRGIN
FORESTS

The forests of the Virgin Islands are rich, biodiverse ecosystems. They range from scrubby, cactus-strewn coastal bushlands to lush, moist tropical habitats, providing shelter to a wide variety of native plants, birds and wildlife. Despite their small size, the islands' forests play a crucial role in conservation and cultural identity, and there are countless ways for visitors to explore.

Atlantic Ocean

BRITISH VIRGIN ISLANDS (UK)

Little Jost Van Dyke

Jost Van Dyke
Great Harbour

US VIRGIN ISLANDS (US)

Great Tobago

Great Thatch

Outer Brass Island

Hans-Lollik Island

Inner Brass Island

Magens Bay

Thatch Cay

Crown Mountain

Savana Island

Charlotte Amalie

St Thomas

Cruz Bay

St John

Cora Bay

Water Island *Hassel Island*

Red Hook

Virgin Islands National Park

Bordeaux Mountain

Saba Island

Great St James Island

Capella Islands

Caribbean Sea

St Thomas' East End
Explore the Mangroves
Adventure-travel companies like Virgin Islands Ecotours can get you out in a kayak exploring the lesser-appreciated mangrove forests that line much of the coast. Then, strap on a snorkel to see all the fish that live in the mangroves' rich ecosystem.

🚗 *5 min west of Red Hook*

▶ p57

Virgin Islands National Park
History Lost to the Jungle
This stunning national park covers two-thirds of St John, offering more than two dozen hiking trails. There are options that will please families, novices and more avid hikers alike. Trek to clifftop overlooks, Taíno petroglyphs, sugar-mill ruins or remote beaches.

🥾 *5 min from Cruz Bay*

▶ p70

Sage Mountain National Park
Lofty Vistas

Stop in at the gift shop for a hand-drawn map of this small but spectacular park on Tortola, which holds the highest point in the Virgin Islands. Ancient gum trees and fanning banana plants line the muddy trails.

🚗 *15 min west of Road Town*

▶ p132

Gorda Peak National Park
Dry Forests

The uppermost slopes of Virgin Gorda lie within the BVI's largest national park, which protects one of the last remaining examples of a Caribbean dry forest. This is the best place to spot a Virgin Gorda gecko, the smallest reptile in the world.

🚗 *10 min north of Spanish Town*

▶ p152

The Baths National Park
Giant Boulders

Scramble through a surreal adult playground on Virgin Gorda. Not only are there giant 40ft boulders strewn across a white-sand beach, there's also a unique ecosystem of dry scrublands peppered with organ pipe cacti.

🚗 *10 min south of Spanish Town*

▶ p150

Mosquito Island
Necker Island
Prickly Pear Island
Leverick Bay
Gorda Peak
Virgin Gorda
The Dogs
Great Camanoe
Guana Island
Scrub Island
Spanish Town
East End
Beef Island
Tortola
Road Town
Cooper Island
Sage Mountain
West End
Sir Francis Drake Channel
Ginger Island
Salt Island
Coral Bay
Peter Island
Caribbean Sea
Norman Island

0 — 10 km
N
0 — 5 miles

LIFE OF
THE PARTY

Drinking in the Virgin Islands centers around relaxed, open-air bars, many of which double as restaurants. Hot nightlife spots include Cruz Bay (St John), Red Hook and Frenchtown (St Thomas), Christiansted (St Croix), Cane Garden Bay (Tortola) and White Bay (Jost Van Dyke). Expect live reggae or calypso music, monthly full-moon parties, local microbrews and iconic island cocktails like the bushwacker.

★ CRAFT BEER

Microbreweries are popping up all around the USVI. Beer from St John Brewers, known for its mango pale ale and hoppy India pale ale, is widely available.

▶ Get to know the breweries of Christiansted (p94)

TOP: DANITA DELIMONT/ALAMY. BOTTOM: VALERIE JOHNSON/SHUTTERSTOCK

Best Nightlife Experiences

▶ **Hoist a drink with the calypso-crooning owner of Foxy's.** (p191)

▶ **Watch as the Red Hook ferry dock bursts alive at sundown.** (p60)

▶ **Groove to live music at the open-air bars of Cane Garden Bay.** (p135)

▶ **Join the yacht circuit at Norman Island.** (p143)

▶ **Watch a drag show in Frederiksted.** (p108)

← FULL-MOON PARTIES

During full moons, band-filled parties rock Tortola and Beef Island. Typically, there's no cover charge: you just buy some food or drinks.

▶ Experience the fun at Trellis Bay (p141)

Top Foxy's (p191) **Bottom** St John Brewers' Island Summer Ale

↘ LOCAL DISHES

Callaloo Spicy soup stirred with okra, various meats, greens and hot peppers.

Pate (pah-tay) Flaky fried dough pockets stuffed with spiced chicken, fish or other meat.

Fungi (foon-ghee) A polenta-like cornmeal cooked with okra, typically topped by fish and gravy.

JEFFREY ISAAC GREENBERG 11+/ALAMY

Best Food Experiences

▶ Dine on fresh-caught lobster, the specialty of remote Anegada. (p172)

▶ Try a roti (burrito-like flat-bread wrap) at Singh's Fast Food in Christiansted. (p113)

▶ Tear into ribs or barbecue chicken at Uncle Joe's BBQ in Cruz Bay. (p86)

▶ Pair conch fritters with rum punch at Pusser's in Road Town. (p123)

CONCH OR CALLALOO?

▬▬▬ Small, unadorned restaurants serving West Indian fare are your best bet for dining in the Virgin Islands. Soups and stews are staples. Meat (chicken, pork and goat) is primarily curried or barbecued with tangy spices. All manner of fish and shellfish (especially conch) make it onto the table alongside mashed or steamed yams and cassavas. Plantains and mangoes are popular, too. When in doubt, eat what the locals are eating!

↓ St John Carnival

Carnival on St John falls over the Fourth of July holiday weekend, luring visitors from the US mainland.

STXPride

STXPride is one of the few Pride celebrations in the West Indies. Events take place each June in Frederiksted.
▶ stcroixpride.org

↑ Full-Moon Parties

With few tourists, locals have more time to relax. See them in action at one of the monthly full-moon parties on Beef Island.
▶ trellisbaymarket.com/fullmoonparty

JUNE

Average daytime max: 88°F
Days of rainfall: 7

JULY

The Virgin Islands in
SUMMER

→ BVI Emancipation Festival

The BVI Emancipation Festival in
Tortola is the biggest cultural fete in the
territory, held over three days in August.
▶ facebook.com/virginislandsfestival

Xmas in July

Xmas in July is a quirky event
where boaters from Puerto
Rico come to Virgin Gorda
for a big bash.
▶ wallycastro.com/xmas-in-july

It's technically hurricane
season, but it won't
reach its peak until
mid-August. Come in
early summer and you'll
likely avoid a storm.

AUGUST

Average daytime max: 89°F
Days of rainfall: 8

Average daytime max: 89°F
Days of rainfall: 9

Packing notes
A wide-brimmed hat,
reef-safe sunscreen
and strong insect
repellant with DEET.

Many USVI hotels produce elaborate dinner celebrations to lure American travelers for the Thanksgiving holidays.

← September is peak hurricane season. There are steep discounts on flights and hotels for those willing to risk a storm.

↗ This is the rainiest time of year – and also the buggiest. It's best to keep flexible with your plans.

SEPTEMBER

Average daytime max: 89°F
Days of rainfall: 12

OCTOBER

The Virgin Islands in
AUTUMN

↘ Anegada Lobster Festival

Each November, the Anegada Lobster Festival draws foodies to the faraway island to gorge on the Caribbean's greatest delicacy.

▶ p172

↓ November marks the start of conch season, when the mollusks are widely available and slathered in butter sauce on local plates.

BVI Fungi Festival

The territory-wide BVI Fungi Festival celebrates the Virgin Islands' unique musical style over three days in November.

NOVEMBER

Average daytime max: 88°F
Days of rainfall: 11

Average daytime max: 86°F
Days of rainfall: 10

🧳 Packing notes

A raincoat or umbrella will help during these rainy months, as will insect repellant.

Crucian Christmas Festival

St Croix throws a big bash to end one year and start the other during the weeks-long Crucian Christmas Festival.

▶ visitusvi.com

← Old Year's Night

There's nowhere better to celebrate New Year's Eve than on Jost Van Dyke at Foxy's famous Old Year's Night celebration.

▶ foxysbar.com

▶ p191

Demand for accommodations peaks during the dry season. View tours and overnight adventures in advance at lonelyplanet.com.

DECEMBER

Average daytime max: 84°F
Days of rainfall: 6

JANUARY

The Virgin Islands in
WINTER

← St John Arts Festival

The St John Arts Festival takes over Cruz Bay for one week of music, craft fairs and film screenings each February.

▶ sjcf.org

→ 8 Tough Miles

8 Tough Miles lures athletes to Virgin Islands National Park for a hilly race from Cruz Bay to Coral Bay each February.

▶ 8tuffmiles.com

Winter is the dry and sunny high season, when everything is open and activities are going full tilt.

FEBRUARY

Average daytime max: 83°F
Days of rainfall: 4

Average daytime max: 84°F
Days of rainfall: 4

🧳 Packing notes

Just in case: a long-sleeved shirt or light jacket for a windy evening.

↓ Hiking is wonderful this time of year as there are fewer people, yet the conditions are still ideal.

Taste of St Croix

Taste of St Croix brings more than 40 local chefs, restaurants and farms to downtown Christiansted each April.

▶ tasteofstcroix.com

It's shoulder season in the Virgin Islands, with great weather, fewer crowds and discounted prices.

MARCH

Average daytime max: 84°F
Days of rainfall: 4

APRIL

The Virgin Islands in
SPRING

↓ St Thomas Carnival

The USVI's biggest bash is the whopping, party-hearty St Thomas Carnival from mid-April to early May.

▶ vicarnivalschedule.com
▶ p54

→ Sailors, swimmers and snorkelers might like April and May best, when the water is at its calmest.

Virgin Gorda Easter Festival

The Virgin Gorda Easter Festival falls over Easter weekend and includes live music, a carnival village and parades.

▶ facebook.com/virgingordaeasterfestival

MAY

Average daytime max: 85°F
Days of rainfall: 6

Average daytime max: 87°F
Days of rainfall: 10

 Packing notes

Sunscreen and a hat, though a smaller rainy season in May makes a raincoat handy.

ST THOMAS & ST CROIX
Trip Builder

TAKE YOUR PICK OF MUST-SEES AND HIDDEN GEMS

The two largest Virgins are well suited for families and those who want more than just a beach to plop down on. There are several forts, themed attractions and rum distilleries. Plus, the dining is the best in the USVI.

🗺️ Trip Notes

Hub towns Charlotte Amalie, Christiansted, Frederiksted

How long Allow 8 days

Getting around Hire a car on both Virgins to go at your own pace. Alternatively, use the cross-island Vitran buses, or safari taxis.

Tips Be sure to time your trip around the interisland ferry schedule; otherwise, you'll need to take expensive seaplanes.

Magens Bay Beach
Spend a full day at one of the Caribbean's most iconic beaches. You can rent kayaks, walk the nature trail and dine right on the sands.
🚗 *15 min from Charlotte Amalie*

Crown Mountain
Savana Island
St Thomas
Charlotte Amalie
Water Island

Charlotte Amalie
Stroll the historic streets of downtown, stopping at Fort Christian, climbing the 99 Steps and shopping for art and souvenirs.
🚗 *15 min from Cyril E King Airport*

Frederiksted
Finish your trip at funky little Frederiksted, making sure to stop at the nearby rum distilleries and craft breweries on the way.
🚗 *30 min from Salt River Bay*

Frederiksted

Ⓝ 0 ————————— 20 km
   0 ————————— 10 miles

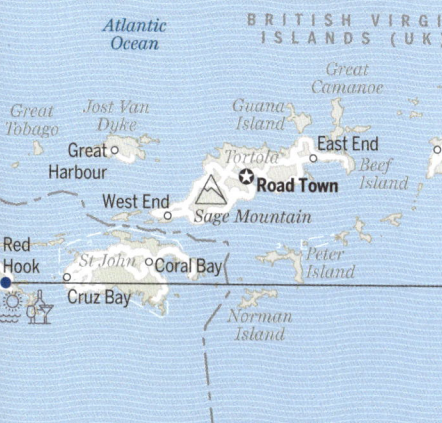

Atlantic Ocean

B R I T I S H   V I R G I N
I S L A N D S   (U K)

Great Tobago

Jost Van Dyke

Great Camanoe

Guana Island

Leverick Bay

Virgin Gorda

Great Harbour

East End

Spanish Town

Tortola

Road Town

Beef Island

West End

Sage Mountain

Red Hook

St John

Coral Bay

Peter Island

Cruz Bay

Norman Island

U S   V I R G I N
I S L A N D S
(U S)

Caribbean Sea

Red Hook
Explore more beaches and mangrove forests on the East End of St Thomas, finishing your day with happy hour in Red Hook.

🚐 *20 min from Charlotte Amalie*

Salt River Bay National Historical Park
Head over to the Salt River Bay National Historical Park to explore the pre-Columbian ruins and kayak the Bio Bay, which glows with bioluminescent plankton at night.

🚗 *20 min from Cane Bay*

Christiansted
Take the two-hour ferry over to Christiansted, then dive into its strong Danish-colonial history. Enjoy a fine meal in the USVI's foodie hub.

⛴ *2 hrs from Charlotte Amalie*

Buck Island

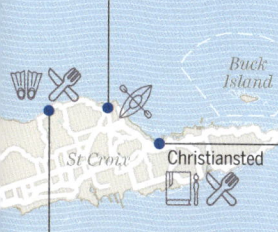

St Croix

Christiansted

Cane Bay
Dive or snorkel at The Wall, a dramatic precipice just off the north coast of St Croix. Then, grab lunch at one of the casual seafront cafes.

🚐 *30 min from Christiansted*

ST JOHN & JOST VAN DYKE
Trip Builder

TAKE YOUR PICK OF MUST-SEES AND HIDDEN GEMS

 Make St John your home base so you can explore the beaches, trails and historic ruins of Virgin Islands National Park. Then, cross into the BVI to escape from it all on neighboring Jost Van Dyke.

Trip Notes

Hub towns Cruz Bay, Coral Bay, Great Harbour

How long Allow 7 days

Getting around You could hire a car for greater flexibility on St John, though active travelers can walk most places, assisted here and there by taxis or the bus. Jost Van Dyke is pretty walkable, and taxis are available.

Tips Be sure to time this trip around the Cruz Bay–Jost Van Dyke ferry, which runs three times per week.

5 km
2.5 miles

Atlantic
Ocean

Great
Tobago

Cruz Bay
Spend your first day exploring lovely little Cruz Bay, grabbing a map for Virgin Islands National Park at the visitor center.
1 hr from Charlotte Amalie, St Thomas

Lovango
Cay

Cruz Bay

Great
St James
Island

Little
St James
Island

US VIRGIN
ISLANDS
(US)

Great Harbour & White Bay
Ferry over to Great Harbour, home to the famous bar and restaurant Foxy's, which has frequent live music. Then, walk over to White Bay, birthplace of the painkiller cocktail.

⚓ *35 min from Cruz Bay*

Bubbly Pool
Hire a taxi (there are boat or land options) for the trip around Jost Van Dyke to the Bubbly Pool, a natural Jacuzzi along the northeastern coast.

🚗 + 🚶 *30 min from White Bay*

North Shore
Spend the next two days either hiking or taking taxis out to North Shore beaches like Honeymoon or Maho Bay.

🚗 *20 min from Cruz Bay*

Coral Bay
Use the quirky frontier outpost Coral Bay as a base for exploring the island's quiet East End and Salt Pond Bay, both of which have great hikes and snorkeling.

🚌 *30 min from Cruz Bay*

Reef Bay Trail
Trek the island's most famous trail, spotting Taíno petroglyphs and colonial-era ruins. Then, visit the most famous ruins of them all: the Annaberg Sugar Plantation.

🚌 *15 min from Cruz Bay*

Majohnny Hill
Little Jost Van Dyke
Jost Van Dyke
White Bay
Great Harbour
Little Harbour
Garner Bay
Green Cay
Sandy Cay

B R I T I S H V I R G I N I S L A N D S (U K)

✪ **Road Town**

Tortola

△ *Sage Mountain*

West End

Frenchmans Cay

Sir Francis Drake Channel

Virgin Islands National Park

Coral Bay

St John

△ *Bordeaux Mountain*

Coral Bay

Caribbean Sea

TORTOLA & THE LITTLE SISTERS
Trip Builder

TAKE YOUR PICK OF MUST-SEES AND HIDDEN GEMS

Explore the varied contours of the largest and most populated island in the BVI from its capital, Road Town, to its jungled peaks, arty shops and low-key beaches. Of course, you can't leave Tortola without day-tripping to the Little Sisters, a haven for marine life just offshore.

🗺 Trip Notes

Hub towns Road Town

How long Allow 1 week

Getting around The best way to make the most of Tortola is to rent a car at the Beef Island airport, or in Road Town. Be advised, however, that roads are steep and tangled.

Tips Boat charters to the Little Sisters can be expensive, so try and gather a big group of fellow travelers. The more people, the cheaper it is for everyone.

Cane Garden Bay
Spend a lazy day at Cane Garden Bay, a lively strip of sand with loungers, beach bars and the Callwood Rum Distillery.
🚗 *20 min from Road Town*

Sage Mountain

Great Thatch

Little Thatch

West End

Frenchmans Cay

West End
Take a trip around the sleepy West End, stopping for lunch at a dockside cafe in Soper's Hole before continuing over to the wide crescent beach at Smuggler's Cove.
🚗 *40 min from Road Town*

US VIRGIN ISLANDS (US)

Sage Mountain
Hike to the highest point in all of the Virgin Islands, exploring the dense forests and sweeping views of Sage Mountain National Park.
🚗 *20 min from Road Town*

Josiah's Bay
Stop at Surf School BVI for boards and a guide; this beach catches year-round swells, making it the perfect spot to learn how to ride waves in the Caribbean.

🚗 *20 min from Road Town*

Atlantic Ocean

Prickly Pear Island

Mosquito Island

Virgin Gorda

△ *Gorda Peak*

George Dog

West Dog *The Dogs*

Great Dog

Guana Island

Great Camanoe

Scrub Island

Little Camanoe

East End

Beef Island

Tortola

❋ **Road Town**

Beef Island
Before you fly out from the airport on Beef Island, be sure to stop by Trellis Bay. Shops here like Aragorn's Studio sell authentic BVI crafts and souvenirs.

🚗 *25 min from Road Town*

Fallen Jerusalem

Sir Francis Drake Channel

Cooper Island

Ginger Island

Salt Island

Dead Chest Island

The Little Sisters
Charter a speedboat to take you on a full-day trip out to the Little Sisters, a chain of smaller islands just south of Tortola that offers sublime snorkeling and diving.

⛴ *1 day from Road Town*

Peter Island

B R I T I S H   V I R G I N
I S L A N D S   (U K)

Norman Island

Road Town
Hobnob with the international financial brokers taking advantage of the biggest city in this tax haven, which holds nice shops and dining.

🚗 *25 min from Terrance B Lettsome Airport*

0 ——— 5 km
0 ——— 2.5 miles

VIRGIN GORDA & ANEGADA
Trip Builder

TAKE YOUR PICK OF MUST-SEES AND HIDDEN GEMS

Really need to get away from it all? If so, Virgin Gorda and Anegada are designed for ultimate relaxation. The former is beloved by high-end jet-setters, while the latter draws wannabe castaways. Paired together, they make a great yin and yang for a laid-back BVI adventure.

🗺️ Trip Notes

Hub towns Spanish Town, The Settlement

How long Allow 1 week

Getting around These islands are small enough that you should be fine with taxis. However, you could rent a car for a day or two to reach further-away attractions.

Tip Time your trip around the Virgin Gorda–Anegada ferry, which departs twice a day, three days per week. The same ferry also services Road Town on Tortola.

Spanish Town
Explore unassuming and spread-out Spanish Town, your point of arrival on Virgin Gorda, before settling into your hotel (likely a fabulous one!).
⛴ *30 min from Terrance B Lettsome Airport*

The Baths
Scramble through turquoise waters on a boulder-strewn beach that will light your Instagram aglow. Then, explore the similarly wild coastline of neighboring Devil's Bay National Park.
🚗 *10 min from Spanish Town*

George Dog
West Dog
Great Dog
Spanish Town
Fallen Jerusalem
Ginger Island
Salt Island *Cooper Island*
Peter Island

Atlantic Ocean

Cow Wreck Bay

Spend your final day on the island's most spectacular beach, either lounging around or getting out into the ocean on a kitesurfing trip.

🚐 *20 min from The Settlement*

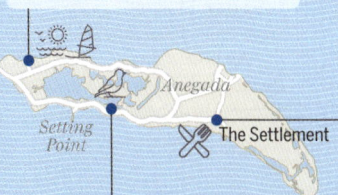

Anegada

Setting Point

The Settlement

The Settlement

Take the long ferry ride up to Anegada, then celebrate your arrival with one of its famed lobster dinners in the only town, known appropriately as The Settlement.

⛴ *1 hr from Spanish Town*

Flamingo Pond

Grab some binoculars! Anegada is the only place in the Virgin Islands where you're practically guaranteed to spot flamingos. The large salt pond on the West End is your best bet.

🚐 *10 min from The Settlement*

Mosquito Island

Necker Island

Prickly Pear Island

Gorda Peak ○ Leverick Bay

Gorda Peak National Park

Virgin Gorda

Gorda Peak

Hike an 8-mile trail through one of the Caribbean's last remaining dry forests, which is filled with native and endangered wildlife.

🚐 *10 min from Spanish Town*

Savannah Bay

Stroll down this wide, sparsely occupied beach, which is one of the few on the island not backed by a luxury resort. The underwater snorkel trail is a real rainbow of marine life.

🚐 *5 min from Spanish Town*

Caribbean Sea

SET SAIL!
Trip Builder

TAKE YOUR PICK OF MUST-SEES AND HIDDEN GEMS

World-class sailing is one of the Virgin Islands' main claims to fame. Clear waters, shipwrecks and secluded coves make for primo snorkeling, while many island bars and restaurants cater specifically to passing boats. Most yachters pick up a catamaran in either St Thomas or Tortola.

🗺 Trip Notes

Hub towns Charlotte Amalie, Cruz Bay, Road Town

How long Allow 2 weeks

Getting around Your boat is your home and mode of transportation. If needed, you can take a taxi from various harbors to pick up supplies.

Tip Check before you book that your boat is allowed to freely cross between the USVI and BVI. Some companies only allow you to charter for one territory or the other.

Cruz Bay, St John
Travel around the south side of St John to Cruz Bay, where you can clear customs back into the USVI and enjoy the lively happy-hour scene.
⚓ 1 day from the Little Sisters

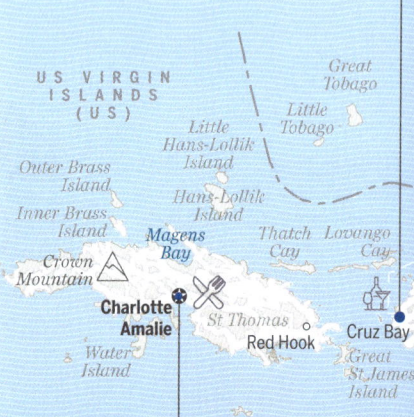

US VIRGIN ISLANDS (US)

Great Tobago

Little Tobago

Little Hans-Lollik Island

Outer Brass Island

Inner Brass Island

Hans-Lollik Island

Magens Bay

Thatch Cay

Lovango Cay

Crown Mountain

Charlotte Amalie

St Thomas

Red Hook

Cruz Bay

Water Island

Great St James Island

Charlotte Amalie, St Thomas
Pick up your boat at one of the yacht harbors near Charlotte Amalie, then use this large town to stock up on supplies for the trip ahead.
🚕 15 min from Cyril E King Airport

White Bay, Jost Van Dyke

Sail over to Jost Van Dyke, anchoring in front of the beach bars at White Bay. The next day, dinghy over to the Bubbly Pool and enjoy an evening of live music at Foxy's.

⛵ ½ day from Tortola

The Baths, Virgin Gorda

Spend a day making footprints on the deserted cays east of Jost Van Dyke before sailing to Virgin Gorda. Anchor at the Baths, and awake to explore the surreal boulder-lined coast.

⛵ 1 day from Jost Van Dyke

The Settlement

Anegada

Atlantic Ocean

B R I T I S H   V I R G I N
I S L A N D S   (U K)

Great Camanoe

The Dogs

Necker Island

Mosquito Island

Prickly Pear Island

Gorda Peak △   ○ Leverick Bay

Jost Van Dyke   *Little Jost Van Dyke*

Guana Island

Serub Island

Beef Island

Virgin Gorda

○ Great Harbour

Tortola

○ East End

○ Spanish Town

Sage Mountain

★ **Road Town**

Sir Francis Drake Channel

West End, Tortola

Clear customs for the BVI at Soper's Hole, a lovely little marina on Tortola's West End where you can have lunch and grab more supplies.

⛵ ½ day from St John

Great Thatch

— West End   *Frenchmans Cay*

Ginger Island

St John

○ Coral Bay

Coral Bay Bordeaux Mountain

Virgin Islands National Park

Peter Island

Salt Island

Cooper Island

Norman Island

Caribbean Sea

Virgin Islands National Park, St John

Sail from St Thomas to St John. Spend the next three days slowly working your way east along the North Shore. Its serene bays have trails leading to virgin forests.

⛵ 1 day from St Thomas

The Little Sisters

Work your way back toward the USVI, stopping at the string of smaller islands known as the Little Sisters, which have amazing snorkeling. Norman Island, in particular, draws a lively yachting crowd.

⛵ 1 day from Virgin Gorda

7 Things to Know About
THE VIRGIN ISLANDS

INSIDER TIPS TO HIT THE GROUND RUNNING

1 A US$-Based Tax Haven

All Virgin Islands use the US dollar as their official currency, making it easy to cross back and forth between both territories. There is no sales tax on goods or services; the stated price on restaurant menus and in shops is what you pay. The BVI's total lack of taxation makes it a major offshore financial center, with a bustling financial services industry centered on Road Town.

2 Tipping Advice

The strong American influence in both territories means that tipping is quite commonplace. A 15% to 20% tip at restaurants is standard, as is a 10% tip on taxi fares. You may also consider tipping US$2 to US$5 per night at hotels for cleaning staff, as well as US$1 per bag for bellhops. Dive or tour boat operators also appreciate recognition for exceptional service. About 15% of the fee is a reasonable baseline.

3 Crossed Signals

Be careful with your cell phone along the USVI–BVI border. Parts of northeastern St John and southwestern Tortola have overlapping signals from the USA and UK, which can lead to expensive roaming charges.

4 Open Containers

Lenient open-container laws mean you can legally walk around with alcoholic beverages on USVI streets. Drinking on a beach in the BVI is similarly allowed – just don't litter.

▶ Read up about safe travel on p204

5 Wild Roads

In both the British and US Virgin Islands you drive on the left-hand side of the road. In fact, the USVI is the only place under the jurisdiction of the USA where this occurs. And yet, since virtually all vehicles are imported from the USA, they tend to have left-side steering. This can take a bit of getting used to, as you never pass another vehicle driver to driver. Also, keep in mind that seatbelts are compulsory in both territories, and children under age five must be in a car seat. The roads on each island pose their own challenges, including potholes, wild curves and incredibly steep hills (particularly on Tortola and St Thomas). Chickens, cows, goats and donkeys often dart in and out of the roadway, to boot. Yet, there's no need rush. On these small islands, nothing is more than an hour away.

6 Local Etiquette

Greetings Greet locals with a 'good morning' or 'good evening' before asking questions or discussing business. Good manners are prized.

Clothing Men without shirts and women in bathing suits or other skimpy attire are frowned upon anywhere apart from the beach.

Time The territories operate on so-called 'island time.' Don't expect things to run like clockwork.

▶ Learn more etiquette on p210

7 Reef-Safe Sunscreen

The USVI passed a law in 2019 banning the sale or usage of common sunscreens with oxybenzone, octocrylene and octinoxate, which can harm coral reefs and disrupt marine ecosystems. Check the ingredient list before purchasing something labeling itself as 'reef safe'; there's a lot of greenwashing in the industry.

▶ See more about responsible travel on p208

US & BRITISH VIRGIN ISLANDS LOCAL TIPS

Read, Listen, Watch & Follow

 READ

Don't Stop the Carnival (Herman Wouk; 1965) Novel based on Wouk's USVI experiences in the 1960s. Jimmy Buffett adapted it into a musical.

Look in the Mirror (Catherine Steadman; 2024) A thriller set in a BVI vacation home where nothing is as it seems.

Not On Any Map (Margie Smith Holt; 2023) A journalist's first-hand account of two Category 5 hurricanes that hit St John in 2017.

Land of Love and Drowning (Tiphanie Yanique; 2014) A saga spanning three decades as St Thomas transitions from Danish to American rule.

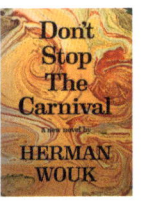
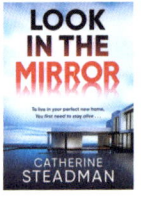
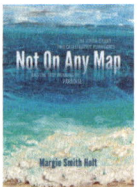

 LISTEN

When Last (The Lashing Dogs; 2000) The album that popularized BVI-style fungi music, known for its unique combo of ukuleles, banjos, bongos and more.

The Fourth Book (Dezarie; 2010) Dreamy beats infuse this downtempo album from a roots reggae star based on St Croix.

Replay (Iyaz; 2010) The chart-topping debut studio album from the BVI's most famous living artist, the R&B legend Iyaz (pictured).

Crucian Scratch Band Music (Blinky & The Roadmasters; 1990) Jazz and calypso influences combine on this classic scratch band album from one of St Croix's most influential groups.

THE PHOTO ACCESS/ALAMY

What Dreams Are Made Of (Rock City; 2015) The best album from hitmaking USVI songwriters behind some of hip-hop's biggest stars, including Rihanna and Nicki Minaj.

WATCH

Weekend at Bernie's II (1993; pictured top)
A black comedy blockbuster set on
St Thomas. It's a sequel to the 1989 hit.

**Paradise Discovered: The Unbreakable
Virgin Islanders** (2018) Documentary
about communities rebuilding after the
devastating 2017 hurricanes.

The Island of Dr Moreau (1977; pictured
bottom) Adapted from HG Wells' novel; a
science fiction horror film shot on St Croix.

Virgin Island (1958) John Cassavetes and
Sidney Poitier star in this BVI-set drama
about fleeing to the tropics.

Timeless: A Virgin Islands Love Story
(2023) First feature-length film shot with
entirely local talent both in front of and
behind the camera.

TRI STAR PICTURES/ALBUM/ALAMY, UNITED ARCHIVES GMBH/ALAMY

FOLLOW

mBlyden vLogs
(youtube.com/c/
mblydenvlogs) Video
blog about Virgin
Islands culture.

Virgin Islands This Week
(facebook.com/Virgin
IslandsThisWeek) The
latest happenings in
the USVI.

British Virgin Islands
(instagram.com/
britishvirginis) Official
Instagram account of
the BVI.

Virgin Islands Life & Style
(vilifeandstyle.com/
magazines) Culture
magazine of the BVI.

VI Now
(vinow.com)
Comprehensive blog
for the USVI.

Sate your
Caribbean
dreaming with
a virtual vacation
at lonelyplanet.
com/caribbean

US VIRGIN ISLANDS

FORTS | BEACHES | RUM

▶ **St Thomas** (p42)

▶ **St John** (p64)

▶ **St Croix** (p88)

Practicalities

DANITA DELIMONT/SHUTTERSTOCK

ARRIVING

Air The USVI's main international airport, **Cyril E King Airport**, is about 3 miles west of Charlotte Amalie on St Thomas. The smaller **Henry E Rohlsen Airport** is on St Croix, about 9 miles southwest of Christiansted.

Boat Cruise ships are big business here, especially on St Thomas. **Havensight** is the busiest of its two terminals, about 1.5 miles east of downtown Charlotte Amalie. The newer **Crown Bay** is a secondary dock, located about 1.5 miles west of Charlotte Amalie.

HOW MUCH FOR A...

national park ticket free

bottle of rum US$12

2-tank dive US$135

GETTING AROUND

Bus Air-conditioned **Vitran** buses (*dpw.vi.gov/about-vitran; US$2 per ride*) operate in the USVI on fixed routes, typically crossing an island from town to town.

Taxi Safari buses are the de facto taxis on St Thomas and St John. These communal, open-air vehicles cost as little as US$1 or US$2 on St Thomas, with more expensive fixed rates on St John from US$3 to US$15, depending on the distance from Cruz Bay.

WHEN TO GO

JAN–MAR
The dry high season is in full swing. Also high: hotel prices.

APR–JUN
There's a slight bump in rainfall, but it's still perfectly pleasant.

JUL–SEP
It's hot, and mostly dry, with a chance of passing hurricanes.

OCT–DEC
The rainiest time of year. Showers typically dissipate by the holidays.

Boat Hourly ferry connections link St Thomas with St John, while daily ferries travel from St Thomas to St Croix. Most BVI islands are accessible by ferry from either St Thomas or St John, with connections most frequent to Tortola.

EATING & DRINKING

The USVI blends traditional West Indian cuisines with American and international fare. That means restaurants will often serve jerked chicken or conch fritters (pictured) alongside pastas, pizzas and burgers. Fish and fungi is the most traditional dish in the USVI, comprised of a polenta-like dumpling, fried fish and okra. You'll find many popular barbecue joints offering grilled chicken, baby back ribs or stewed oxtail alongside rice and beans, coleslaw and macaroni salad. Vegetarians and vegans should look for Rastafarian restaurants serving plant-based Ital foods.

Best rum tasting
Cruzan Rum Distillery
(p95; pictured)

Must-try vegan fare
Ital in Paradise (p113)

CONNECT & FIND YOUR WAY

Wi-fi Internet is widely available and free in many tourist attractions.

Navigation Ferries are integral to exploring the Virgin Islands, so plan excursions around the latest schedules. The **VI Port Authority** (*viport.com*) maintains an updated list. Alternatively, many groups hire a boat and captain for day trips where you can snorkel, swim and drink across the chain.

SAFETY

While the USVI has one of the highest murder rates in the world, according to the UN Office on Drugs and Crime, it rarely directly affects visiting tourists.

WHERE TO STAY

Guesthouses, hotels, private villas and condo resorts are all abundant. High season is mid-December through April, when rooms are costly and reservations essential. Three-night minimum-stay requirements are common.

Town/Area	Pros/Cons
Charlotte Amalie	Charming, history-filled hub on St Thomas with great shopping and dining.
East End	The eastern half of St Thomas is home to the USVI's ritziest beach resorts, some of which are all-inclusive.
Cruz Bay	Low-key B&Bs dominate St John's main town; you'll find camping nearby in Virgin Islands National Park.
Coral Bay	Stunning villas dot the hills above this sleepy town, which is adjacent to the national park.
Christiansted	Central St Croix spot with great dining and nightlife, though no direct beach access.
Frederiksted	St Croix's second city is quirky and gay-friendly, with hotels right on the beach.

MONEY

The USVI runs on American dollars, and there are ATMs in the three main towns. Credit cards are widely accepted. Hotels, restaurants and supermarkets are all more expensive than the continental US. Cocktails, by contrast, are cheaper.

ST THOMAS

SHOPPING | TROPICAL COCKTAILS | VIRGIN BEACHES

RESEARCHED BY MARK JOHANSON

- ▶ **Trip Builder** (p44)
- ▶ **Practicalities** (p45)
- ▶ **Stroll Around Historic Charlotte Amalie** (p46)
- ▶ **Sun, Sand & Sea: Pick Your Beach** (p48)
- ▶ **Escape to the 'Fourth' Virgin** (p52)
- ▶ **Jump Up for Carnival** (p54)
- ▶ **Take a Hike on the West End** (p56)
- ▶ **Local Souvenirs** (p58)
- ▶ **One Night in Red Hook** (p60)
- ▶ **Listings** (p62)

Atlantic
Ocean

Take a hike to a
double-sided **West
End beach** (p56).

🚗 *30 min from
Charlotte Amalie*

Laze away the day on
the beach at **Magens
Bay** (p49).

🚗 *15 min from
Charlotte Amalie*

Enjoy a rum-fueled
evening in the bars of
Red Hook (p60).

🚗 *20 min from
Charlotte Amalie*

*Little
Hans-Lollik
Island*

*Outer Brass
Island*

*Hans-Lollik
Island*

*Dutcheap
Cay*

*Inner Brass
Island*

Salt Cay *West
Cay*

*Crown
Mountain*

*Magens
Bay*

*Thatch
Cay*

*Grass
Cay*

*Savana
Island*

**Charlotte
Amalie**

*Hassel
Island*

Red Hook

*Great
St James
Island*

Travel to the 'fourth'
US Virgin Island,
Water Island (p52).

⛴ *15 min from
Charlotte Amalie*

*Saba
Island*

*Water
Island*

*Little
St James
Island*

*Caribbean
Sea*

Stroll the historic
alleyways and galleries
of downtown **Charlotte
Amalie** (p48; pictured).

🚗 *15 min from Cyril
E King Airport*

*Capella
Islands*

ST THOMAS
Trip Builder

▬▬ Most visitors arrive in the USVI via St Thomas,
and the place knows how to make an impression.
Jungly cliffs poke high into the sky, red-hipped roofs
blossom over hills, and all around the turquoise,
yacht-dotted sea laps a pristine shore.

Practicalities

ARRIVING

Cruise ships take advantage of the same protected harbor that brought the Dutch West India Company here centuries ago. **Cyril E King Airport**, the region's main air hub, is just west of Charlotte Amalie.

FIND YOUR WAY

Keep track of cruise traffic. The more ships in port, the more difficult it can be to find a safari bus.

MONEY

St Thomas is the most commercialized – and expensive – of the Virgins; credit cards are widely accepted.

WHERE TO STAY

Area	Pros/Cons
Charlotte Amalie	Smaller and more casual guesthouses than found elsewhere, though it gets pretty deserted at nightfall.
East End	Big, beachfront resorts are the primary option east of Charlotte Amalie, alongside high-end condo rentals.
Water Island	A rare glamping option offers peace, solitude and lower prices.

EATING & DRINKING

St Thomas has a wide mix of American and West Indian cuisines. To get a real taste of the islands, stick to the latter. Johnnycakes (fried dough snacks; pictured top), conch fritters (made from the local mollusks), callaloo (a leafy green; pictured bottom) and saltfish (typically cod) are regional delicacies.

Best locals-only spot
Daylight Bakery & Diamond Barrel Restaurant (p62)

Must-try fusion food
Gladys' Cafe (p62)

GETTING AROUND

Ferry St Thomas has excellent ferry connections to other Virgins. The two main marine terminals are at Charlotte Amalie (to the BVI and St Croix) and Red Hook (to St John).

Safari bus
These open-air communal taxis with benches hold up 20 people. Flag them down by flapping your hand. The fare is US$1 or US$2.

ST THOMAS FIND YOUR FEET

JAN–MAR
It's drier, cooler, and the best time of year to visit.

APR–JUN
Carnival season on St Thomas brings food fairs and street parades.

JUL–SEP
Low season brings hotel discounts, but also potential tropical storms.

OCT–DEC
Rains are more frequent, but die down by the year's end.

01

Stroll Around Historic
CHARLOTTE AMALIE

ART | HISTORY | SHOPPING

With two to six Love Boats docking in town daily, Charlotte Amalie (*a-mall-ya*) is one of the most popular cruise-ship destinations in the Caribbean. Downtown buzzes with visitors swarming cafes, jewelry shops and boutiques, making it great for a leisurely stroll.

SANDRA FOYT/SHUTTERSTOCK

🗺 How to

Getting around Safari-style taxis holding up to 20 people ply the streets here. Flag one down by flapping your hand. The fare is US$1 or US$2.

Getting oriented Charlotte Amalie stretches about 2.5 miles around Charlotte Amalie Harbor from **Havensight** on the east to **Frenchtown** on the west.

Cruise docks Cruises dock at either Havensight or **Crown Bay** (pictured); the latter is one bay to the west of Charlotte Amalie, not far from Frenchtown.

🚶 The Step Streets

The famed 99 Steps is one of several 'step streets' that rise up from the harbor at Charlotte Amalie. The **St Thomas Historical Trust** (*stthomas historicaltrust.org*) has been raising funds to restore more of these stair-like streets, which date from the Danish era when town planners created roads up hillsides too steep for horse-drawn carts.

03 Grab a snack at **MBW Cafe & Bakery**, an NGO that gives visitors a chance to support at-risk youth while sampling local goodies like rum cakes and banana bites.

04 The **St Thomas Synagogue** is the second-oldest synagogue in the US. The current building dates from 1833, but Jews have worshipped here since 1796. There's a tiny museum in the back.

02 Climb the famed **99 Steps** from Kongens Gade up into a canopy of trees at the foot of Blackbeard's Castle, where there's an impressive view. The 18th-century steps are made from ship-ballast brick.

05 Cap off the walk at **Taphus Beer House**, which boasts exposed stone walls, a horseshoe-shaped mahogany bar and a rotating list of craft beers, including St Thomas's own Frenchtown Brewing.

01 Start at the brick-red **Fort Christian**, the oldest Danish fortification in the Caribbean, dating to 1672. Over the years it has housed a jail, governor's residence and Lutheran church.

Charlotte Amalie Harbor

Emancipation Garden

Crystal Gade

Commandant Gade

Garden St

Kongens Gade

Raadets Gade

Nye Gade

Wimmelskafts Gade (Back St)

Dronningens Gade

(Main St)

Post Office Al

Talbod Gade

Vendors' Plaza

Waterfront Hwy

Fortet Strade

Norre Gade (North St)

Lille Fortet Strade

(Veterans Dr)

Hospital Gade

0

0

200 m

0.1 miles

N

02 Sun, Sand & Sea:
PICK YOUR BEACH

BEACHES | SNORKELING | SURFING

There are some 40 virgin beaches on St Thomas, and they're the main draw for most visitors to the island. Whether you've come to surf, snorkel or suntan, there's a perfect crescent of sand to meet your needs.

🗺️ **How to**

Getting around Safari buses or taxis in Charlotte Amalie can get you out to most beaches, though a car is ideal for hopping around.

Rentals Busier beaches have water-sports outfitters renting snorkel gear, kayaks, paddleboards, surf boards and any other supplies you may need.

Fees Most beaches on St Thomas are free, with the exception of Magens Bay Beach and Lindquist Beach, which both charge a US$5 fee.

The Star Attractions

The sugary mile that fringes **Magens Bay** (*magensbayauthority.com*), 3 miles north of Charlotte Amalie, makes almost every travel publication's list of beautiful beaches. The seas here are calm, the bay broad and the surrounding green hills dramatic; tourists mob the place to soak it all up. Magens Bay Beach has lifeguards, picnic tables, changing facilities, a taxi stand, food vendors, and water-sports operators renting kayaks, paddleboards and paddleboats.

Out east, **Lindquist Beach** is part of the protected Smith Bay Park and is the only beach other than Magens with an entry fee. This narrow strand off Smith Bay Rd is a real stunner: calm, true-blue water laps the soft white sand, while several cays shimmer in the distance. Hollywood has, for good reason,

🐟 **Reef-Safe Sunscreen**

In the USVI, it's illegal to purchase or use sunscreen that is not safe for coral reefs. This ban went into effect in 2020 and primarily covers products that include toxic ingredients like oxybenzone, octinoxate and octocrylene. Read labels closely before purchasing; many products calling themselves 'reef friendly' are anything but.

Top left and above Magens Bay
Left Lindquist Beach

filmed several commercials here. There's a lifeguard, picnic tables and a bathhouse with showers, but no other amenities. It's a lower-key alternative to Magens, and lovely for a swim.

Top Snorkel Spots

Coki Beach lies on a protected cove at the entrance to the Coral World Ocean Park (which, for animal welfare reasons, is not recommended). The snorkeling at Coki is excellent, with lots of fish action, and you can swim from the shore with gear from the on-site rental shops. This narrow beach fills up with locals and tourists enjoying the eateries, hair-braiding vendors and loud music. A festive scene results. However, Coki is the one beach on St Thomas with touts – as soon as you arrive someone will quickly become your 'friend.'

Two bays east, **Sapphire Beach** is among St Thomas's prettiest white-sand beaches,

How to Beach-Hop the Island

The best way to get around St Thomas is to either establish a relationship with a taxi driver or rent a vehicle. The roads are a maze, and local knowledge comes in handy when making your way from Charlotte Amalie to Red Hook or one of the many beaches. Mapping apps are notoriously unreliable here, too. Safari buses will theoretically take you around the island for a few dollars. In practice, though, they are often converted into island tours when cruise ships arrive. This effectively renders the default public transportation on the island out of service until ships depart again.

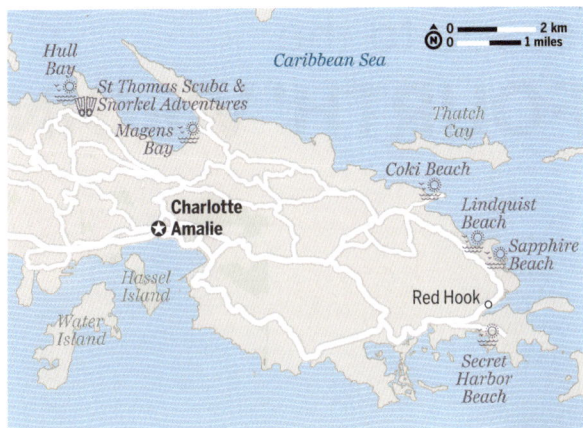

Left Safari bus **Below** Coki Beach

and accordingly it draws a big tourist crowd. Amenities include water-sports rentals (paddle-boards, snorkel gear, kayaks), bathrooms and a bar-restaurant. There's good snorkeling on the reef to the right of the beach.

For a more low-key snorkel spot, consider **Secret Harbor Beach**. Small and hammock-strewn, this west-facing beach in front of the eponymous resort could hardly be more tranquil. It's an excellent place to snorkel with equipment rented from the resort's water-sports operation. Bathrooms and food are available, too.

Surfs Up!

On the north coast and just west of Magens Bay, **Hull Bay** is usually a gem of solitude when Magens is overrun. The shady strand lies at the base of a steep valley and has two fun restaurant-bars but no other facilities. It's a locals' beach: fishers anchor their small boats here and dogs lope around. When there's a northern swell, Hull Bay is also the best surf beach around. **St Thomas Scuba & Snorkel Adventures** (*stthomas adventures.com*), located at Hull Bay, rents surfboards and paddleboards and leads terrific night snorkel tours. It also offers a slew of other snorkeling, diving, kayaking and hiking jaunts around the island.

FROM LEFT: RAKSYBH/SHUTTERSTOCK, SANDRA FOYT/SHUTTERSTOCK

03

Escape to the
'FOURTH' VIRGIN

COCKTAILS | BEACHES | GOLF CARTS

Cheekily dubbed the 'fourth' US Virgin Island by some, and scoffed at by others, Water Island feels more Florida panhandle than Caribbean, but is still a worthy day trip for visitors seeking a lazy beach day. Just a 15-minute ferry ride from Crown Bay Marina in St Thomas, it offers a peaceful break from Charlotte Amalie's high energy.

🗺 How to

Getting here Around the peninsula from French-town lies Crown Bay, a cruise-ship-filled marina that's the jumping-off point for the **Water Island Ferry** (waterislandferry.com). It leaves hourly and costs US$20 round trip.

Getting around Golf carts are available, though the island is easily walkable by foot.

What to bring Purchase all the supplies you'll need for the day in Charlotte Amalie, as there are no shops on Water Island.

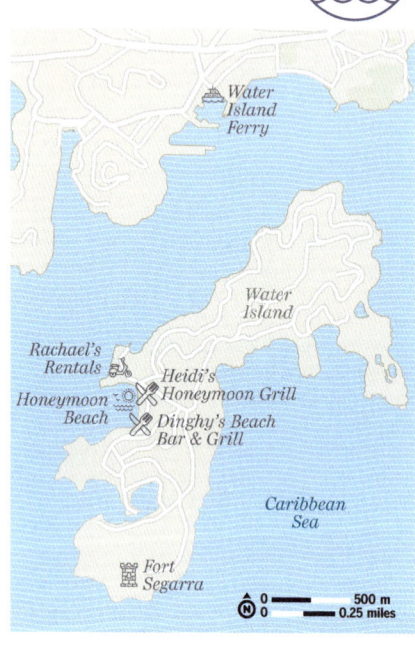

Water Island is home to a smattering of activities that offer many beachgoers an idyllic view of the Caribbean. Namely: white-sand beaches and an island where the primary modes of transportation are flip-flops and golf carts.

As soon as you step off of the ferry dock at Phillips Landing, you'll see the golf carts for hire. **Rachael's Rentals** (rachaelsrentals. com) has carved out a niche by loaning visitors this minia-ture means of transportation for more than a decade. The staff are friendly enough and the rates really aren't that bad. However, unless you're determined to reach the remnants of a 20th-century battery and bunkers at **Fort Segarra**, it's wise to forgo the golf cart and walk the 15 min-utes to **Honeymoon Beach**.

Plop down beneath a palm tree – as long as you're alert to falling coconuts – or slide into a chair at **Dinghy's**

SOLARISYS/SHUTTERSTOCK

🏰 A Fort Like No Other

Water Island's Fort Segarra is unusual among Caribbean forts. Though colonial-era fortifications rise along key ports on most islands, this one is actually a product of WWII. Designed to protect a US Navy submarine base on St Thomas, the majority of Segarra lies underground. The war ended before the fort was completed, but Fort Segarra's lingering subterranean chambers and tunnels are open for visitors. There are also watch towers, barracks and gun emplacements. Be warned, however, that the fort was used between 1948 and 1950 as a chemical test site and is monitored by the US Army Corps of Engineers to ensure no residual contamination remains.

Beach Bar & Grill (*dinghys beachbar.com*) for a better-than-average tuna tartare and an excellent rum cocktail. Just offshore, a small armada of catamarans are likely to be moored outside of a swim area, which features a convenient floating raft that draws the eye of curious green and hawksbill turtles munching on sea grass. On the way back to the dock, be sure to swing by **Heidi's Honeymoon Grill** (*facebook. com/heidishoneymoon*) for its famous fish tacos before setting a timer to catch the last ferry back to St Thomas by 6pm.

Above Honeymoon Beach

Jump Up for Carnival

THE BIGGEST CULTURAL EVENT OF THE YEAR

American author Hunter S Thompson wrote of the St Thomas Carnival in his cult novel *The Rum Diary* as a riotous amalgam of pagan and Christian rites where overt sexuality and religious catharsis go hand in hand. Little has changed in the ensuing 60 years, as this month-long bash rages on larger and louder than ever.

Billed as the second-biggest Carnival in the Caribbean (after the one in Port of Spain, Trinidad), the annual fete spans beauty contests, boat races, food fairs, calypso competitions and steel-pan jamborees. A Carnival Village in downtown Charlotte Amalie hosts dozens of food stalls, makeshift bars, glowing carnival rides and nightly live entertainment. Key events in the final week (usually late April or early May) include J'ouvert, an alcohol-fueled street party that kicks off at 4am, runs well past sunrise, and features lots of twerking. The more family-friendly Adults Parade is a whirlwind of feathers and sequins that culminates in fireworks over Charlotte Amalie's harbor and the end of Carnival.

The performance line-up for the stage at Carnival Village typically includes some of the biggest names in Caribbean music, such as Shabba Ranks, Kes or Shaggy. Expect reggae, soca and calypso tunes to blast from USVI vehicles and emanate from shops, restaurants and beach bars. Similarly, *quelbe* and *fungi* (foon-ghee, also an island food made of cornmeal) are two types of commonly heard folk music. *Quelbe* blends jigs, quadrilles, military fife and African drum music with (often bitingly satirical) lyrics from the field songs of enslaved people. *Fungi* uses homemade percussion instruments such as washboards, ribbed gourds and conch shells to accompany a singer.

St John Carnival & the Christmas Festival

There are separate Carnival celebrations on St John and St Croix, which take place on entirely different dates. Though smaller by comparison, these fests can be more approachable for the first-time celebrant.

Left Charlotte Amalie **Center** Cruz Bay **Right** St Thomas Carnival dancer

Check **VI Carnival Schedule** *(vicarnivalschedule.com)* to see the dates and times.

The St John Carnival, in Cruz Bay, falls around Emancipation Day (July 3) and US Independence Day (July 4), drawing holiday vacationers from the US mainland. There's a food fair, parade, beauty pageant, fireworks and, of course, plenty of feathers and sequins. Over on St Croix, Carnival season is two weeks of pageants, parades and calypso competitions putting a West Indies spin on the Christmas holidays. The main event of this Carnival, also called the Crucian Christmas Festival, is the Adults Parade, which falls on Three Kings Day (January 6) and culminates in an evening of fireworks.

> Expect to see plenty of *moko jumbies*, the iconic stilt walkers.

In all Carnival celebrations, expect to see plenty of *moko jumbies*, the iconic stilt walkers featured on the logo of the US Virgin Islands Department of Tourism. These colorfully dressed dancers are not only highly trained performers, but also cultural icons with roots tracing back to West Africa. Their presence at the Carnival is said to be a good omen.

Carnival Vibes Outside Carnival Season

No matter the season, you can still experience the food, music and dancing of Carnival at island bars, restaurants and resorts. Many hotels host musicians for live music on certain evenings during the week. Full-moon parties are another good bet for local music and dancing, particularly in the neighboring BVI. Jump ups (mini music-filled street carnivals) also take place four times a year on St Croix, usually for one night only in February, May, July and November.

The Arts Scene in Charlotte Amalie

'Visit **Creative Native** *(thecreativenative.art)*, on the corner of Dronningens Gade and Stor Tvaer Gade. Ama Dennis is the artist. She's driven by her passion for her home and creates compelling artistic narratives that preserve our culture. It is a unique venue with hand-painted floors and rubble masonry walls that showcase Ama's vivid photographs. Nearby, **81C** *(81cvi. com)* is an art gallery, cafe, wine bar and event venue all in one. **Mystic By the Sea** *(palmpassagevi.com/mystic-by-the-sea)* in Palm Passage is a great gift shop for local art and fair-trade products.'

Recommended by **Anna Monica Villa**, who runs tours for the St Thomas Historical Trust *(stthomas historicaltrust.org)* and Stjernegaard Rejser *(stjerne gaard-rejser.dk; in Danish)*.

04 Take a Hike on the WEST END

HIKING | BEACHES | VIEWS

Avid hikers should head out to St Thomas' lesser-explored West End, where the resorts are few and the hiking trails many. Can't-miss adventures here include the trek up the Brewers Bay Trail and the scramble out to the double-sided beach at Mermaid's Chair. Both hikes offer sweeping views and the chance to cool off in the ocean.

NANCY PAUWELS/SHUTTERSTOCK

🗺 How to

Getting here The **Vitran bus** (*dpw.vi.gov*) can get you out to Brewers Bay or close to Botany Bay, but a car will make things much easier.

When to go For the Mermaid's Chair hike, it's important to time your arrival around low tide.

What to wear Closed-toe shoes are a must for these trails, which go over roots and rocks, and can be slippery when wet.

SEAN PAVONE/SHUTTERSTOCK

Far left top View of Brewers Bay
Far left bottom Brewers Bay beach
Left Mermaid's Chair

Start your West End adventure at **Brewers Bay beach**, which is located just behind the airport next to the University of the Virgin Islands. There are restroom facilities and snack vans serving *pates* (meat-filled dough pockets) or cold Heineken beers. Look for the ruins of the old John Brewer's Estate, where an arrow will guide you to the **Brewers Bay Trail**. The path is really more of a boulder-lined creek bed, which ascends several hundred feet above the sands to John Brewer's Cave, a rocky outcrop shrouded in legends of buried treasure.

Today, the trail is as rugged as it was nearly a century ago, though arrows help hikers climb over smooth boulders, hulking gum trees and floating air plants before making the final push to the top, aided by ropes. It's approximately one hour to ascend and slightly less to descend.

The chance to put one foot in the Caribbean, then another in the Atlantic, is what lures intrepid travelers further west to the remote double-sided beach known as **Mermaid's Chair**. This small strip of sand on the wild western tip of St Thomas is best viewed at low tide. To reach it, plan to hike about 1.3 miles downhill from the Preserve at Botany Bay on a mostly paved road with extensive views over the westerly cays. Just remember: what goes down must come up again!

More Island Adventures

Virgin Islands Ecotours (*viecotours.com*) is St Thomas' premier adventure travel company with a focus on hiking, snorkeling and kayaking. Its signature outing is a three-hour guided kayaking-and-snorkeling expedition where you paddle through a mangrove lagoon to a beach, go for a short hike to a blowhole and then snorkel out to a small shipwreck. Birding and turtle-spotting trips are also available, as are charters. DIY travelers can rental kayaks and stand-up paddleboards (SUPs). The St Thomas headquarters is near Red Hook, but there are a wide array of island-specific tours offered on St John and St Croix, too.

Local Souvenirs

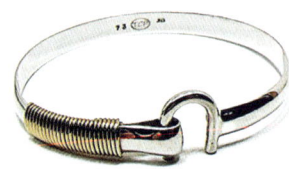

01 Hook Bracelet
Virgin Islanders wear these 'hook bracelets' like wedding rings. If the hook is facing outward, it means you're single.

02 Cruzan Rum
This is the official rum of the USVI and a staple on every bar menu. Use it for rum punch or a painkiller.

03 Blind Betty's Hot Sauce
Vinegar-based pepper sauces are big business in the Virgin Islands. The hotter the better!

04 National Park Tote
These canvas beach totes from Friends of Virgin Islands National Park help support island conservation projects.

05 Recycled Glass Art
The Virgin Islands have a long tradition of recycling glass bottles into art, much of which is inspired by the sea.

06

08

07

10

09

06 Calabash Bowls
Carving patterns into dried calabash gourds is an old West Indian art form brought over from Africa.

07 Crucian Baskets
Basketmaking is a tradition often passed down from mothers to daughters. It is most vibrant on St Croix.

08 Nutmeg Grater
To make the painkiller, a locally famous rum cocktail, you'll need a nutmeg grater. It works great for cinnamon, too!

09 St John VI Pottery
These ceramics inspired by the shapes and colors of Virgin Islands National Park make excellent souvenirs.

10 Mutiny Island Vodka
British plantation owners introduced breadfruit to the Caribbean as a cheap food source for enslaved people. Now, it's distilled into vodka.

05

One Night in
RED HOOK

DINING | DRINKING | DANCING

The dockside bars and restaurants of Red Hook can be deceiving in the heat of the midday sun. At this hour, the place looks downright sleepy; a smattering of coffee shops, gift stores and fishing tackle centers offer the only signs of life. Then, the night falls, the lights turn on, the kitchens fire up and Red Hook becomes *the* epicenter of nightlife.

RICK STRANGE/ALAMY

🗺 **How to**

Getting here St Thomas' biggest resorts lie on the East End not far from Red Hook; all hotels can arrange taxis.

When to go Nightlife begins, in earnest, at happy hour (3pm–6pm) when things get pumping along the waterfront.

Stay safe Red Hook is generally a safe place to be in the evening, but don't wander off alone from there. Take a cab to get back to your lodging.

SANDRA FOYT/SHUTTERSTOCK

Far left top American Yacht Harbor
Far left bottom Red Hook ferry
terminal **Left** View of Red Hook

Charlotte Amalie is the place to be on St Thomas during the daytime, but it's tiny, unassuming Red Hook that tends to rule the night. Yes, it may be more of a glorified ferry dock than an actual town, but there's a small collection of quirky restaurants and themed bars that give the area a well-deserved reputation for letting the good times roll.

Kick the night off at the American Yacht Harbor in the **Island Time Pub** (*facebook.com/IslandTimePub*), where happy hour starts early at 3pm. You can sit at the open-air bar and watch as boats sail into Vessup Bay for the evening. Then, curb your appetite with the renowned snapper piccata at **Pesce Italian** (*pescevi.com*). Or, try the seafood at **Tarpon's Table** (*tarponstable.com*), which serves shrimp po' boy sandwiches, fish tacos and fresh lobster at harborfront tables.

Finish the evening at **Duffy's Love Shack** (*duffyslove shack.com*), a colorful tiki bar famous for its live music, tropical cocktails and up-tempo vibes. Duffy's likes to call itself 'the best parking lot bar in the world,' and energetic DJs do keep the asphalt dance floor grooving until the wee hours. Of all the spots in Red Hook, this has the most history behind it (over three decades). It also tends to draw the largest West Indian crowd, giving it a strong local flavor. Try the signature drink, 'lime in dee coconut,' which includes coconut water, rum and lime juice.

A Slave House Gets a New Life

13 Wimmelskafts Slave House (*13wimmelskafts. com*) is a newly restored enslaved persons and servants quarters from the early 1800s. The structure houses an assortment of artifacts dating back to Pre-Columbian times. The collection includes Taíno carvings, original maps, coins and letters dating back hundreds of years from early colonists and reaching into the modern era. There is an on-site rum distillery, tasting room and also a lush tropical garden to relax. Sample locally made rum, locally roasted coffee and other local foods at the cafe.

Recommended by **Michael Motylinski**, master distiller and owner of Blue Mango Tours. *bluemangotours.com*

Listings

BEST OF THE REST

 More History in Charlotte Amalie

Emancipation Garden

This is where the emancipation proclamation was read after enslaved people were freed on St Croix in 1848. Carnival celebrations and concerts take place here, but mostly folks kick back under trees with smoothies from the Vendors' Plaza next door.

Frederick Evangelical Lutheran Church

During the 19th century, the church had segregated congregations – one West Indian, the other Danish. Now, it's open sporadically during the week, and you can attend services on Sundays.

Government House

Ascend the hill behind the church and you'll come to a grand white mansion housing the territorial governor's offices. It was built between 1865 and 1867, and restored in 1994. There's a pretty little park with a fountain and benches.

 Explore Frenchtown

Frenchtown

The island's 'Frenchies,' aka Huguenots who emigrated to St Thomas from St-Barthélemy during the mid-19th century, populated this fishers' community of brightly painted frame houses on Charlotte Amalie's western edge. Nowadays it has several good restaurants that overlook the water.

Frenchtown Brewing

This brewery is indeed micro: it's only open Monday to Friday, and only brews a handful of ales. Beer buffs will want to seek out the Belgian-style Frenchie Farmhouse Saison and Hop Alley IPA. Tours available by appointment.

 Caribbean Flavors

Daylight Bakery & Diamond Barrel $

It's mostly locals who visit this friendly spot at Charlotte Amalie's edge. If you can get past the guava tarts, sugar cakes and dumb bread, then pans of okra, fish stew, fungi and other island staples await.

Iggie's Oasis $$

Set in a large open-air pavilion overlooking the broad shore at Bolongo Bay Beach Resort, festive Iggie's is beloved for its conch fritters with Creole remoulade, rum-soaked VooDoo Juice and live music most evenings.

Gladys' Cafe $$

With the stereo blaring beside her, Gladys belts out Tina Turner tunes while serving some of the best West Indian food around. Locals and tourists pile in for her callaloo (spicy soup with okra, meats and greens), fungi, ole wife (triggerfish) and fried plantains.

SANDRA FOYT/SHUTTERSTOCK

Emancipation Garden

Old Stone Farmhouse $$$

The 200-year-old farmhouse – once the stable for a nearby sugar plantation – sits high on a hill overlooking St Thomas' only golf course. The menu changes, but local seafood (lobster, mahi-mahi) is always available, as well as a vegetarian option.

Art Galleries & Shops

Mango Tango

The VI's top gallery is far removed in both quality and distance from its downtown brethren. Intricate Haitian metal pieces and contemporary paintings from Washington-based Mel McCuddin are on display alongside the work of the best local painters and potters.

Tillett Gardens

This colorful artists' colony near Tutu Park Mall lures hippies, thinkers, musicians and outcasts with its good-times vibe and welcoming spirit as artists work in their studios. There are also bars, cafes, restaurants and a hostel.

Yacht Haven Grande

Next door to Havensight is this marina and chic shop complex with several waterfront bistros. You can sip cosmos and watch megayachts drift into dock.

AH Riise

This is the famous mall that most cruise visitors beeline to. Here you can buy everything from watches and jewels to tobacco and liquor.

Float Through the Tropical Air

Paradise Point Skyride

Gondolas whisk visitors 700ft up Flag Hill to a scenic outlook. At the top a restaurant, a bar, a gallery of shops and a short nature trail await. A chocolatey bushwacker is the drink of choice while taking in the view.

Paradise Point Skyride

Tree Limin' Extreme

Guides whisk you through the jungle canopy here via zipline. The ride is relatively tame and provides great views of the island-dotted seascape.

Breathe

This nonprofit donation-based yoga studio in Havensight runs daily classes including slow flow, salsa dancing and writer's workshops. All will have your mind floating into the clouds.

A Floating Restaurant?

Pizza Pi VI

Food trucks are so last decade. There are few parts of the world where a 'food boat' is the most popular eatery around. Such is the case with Pizza Pi, a floating restaurant in Christmas Cove with three seasonal menus of New York–style pies.

ST JOHN

SNORKELING | HISTORIC RUINS | VIRGIN FORESTS

RESEARCHED BY MARK JOHANSON

▶ **Trip Builder** (p66)

▶ **Practicalities** (p67)

▶ **Fall for 'Love City'** (p68)

▶ **Hikes in Virgin Islands National Park** (p70)

▶ **The Animals of the Virgin Islands** (p74)

▶ **Hiking the Reef Bay Trail** (p76)

▶ **A Brief History of the USVI** (p78)

▶ **Beach-Hop the North Shore** (p80)

▶ **Hiking & Snorkeling Near Coral Bay** (p82)

▶ **A Private Island Experience** (p84)

▶ **Listings** (p86)

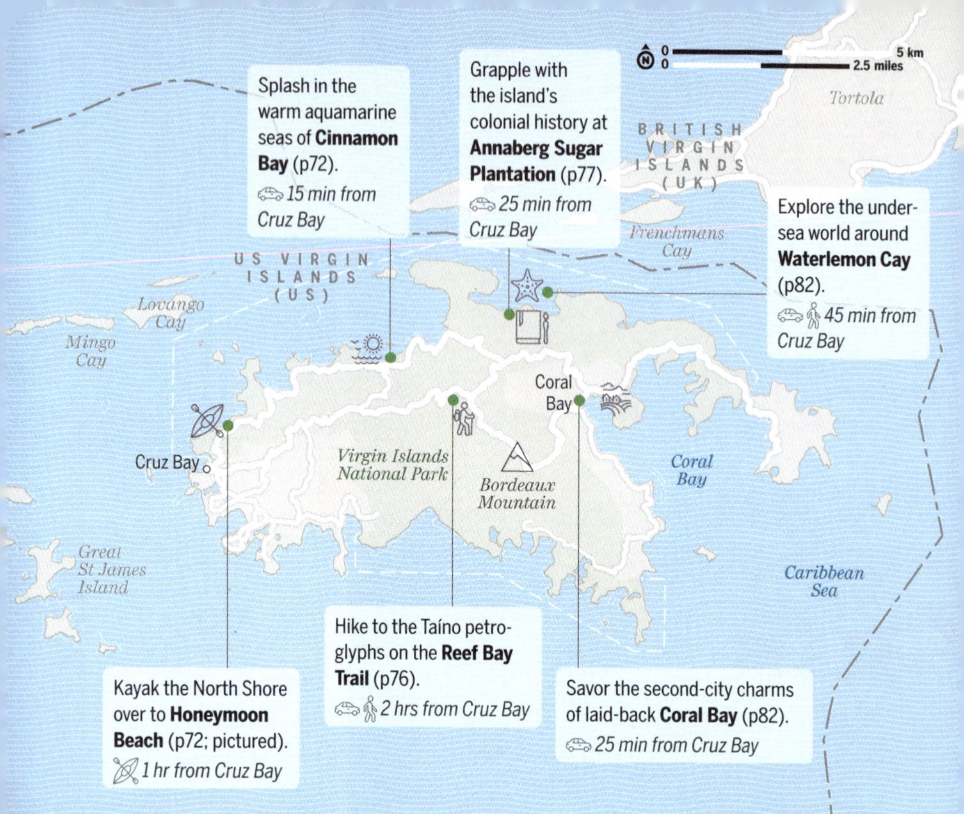

Splash in the warm aquamarine seas of **Cinnamon Bay** (p72).
🚐 *15 min from Cruz Bay*

Grapple with the island's colonial history at **Annaberg Sugar Plantation** (p77).
🚐 *25 min from Cruz Bay*

Explore the undersea world around **Waterlemon Cay** (p82).
🚐🚶 *45 min from Cruz Bay*

Tortola

B R I T I S H
V I R G I N
I S L A N D S
(U K)

Frenchmans Cay

U S   V I R G I N
I S L A N D S
(U S)

Lovango Cay

Mingo Cay

Coral Bay

Cruz Bay

Virgin Islands National Park

Bordeaux Mountain

Coral Bay

Great St James Island

Caribbean Sea

Kayak the North Shore over to **Honeymoon Beach** (p72; pictured).
🛶 *1 hr from Cruz Bay*

Hike to the Taíno petroglyphs on the **Reef Bay Trail** (p76).
🚗🚶 *2 hrs from Cruz Bay*

Savor the second-city charms of laid-back **Coral Bay** (p82).
🚐 *25 min from Cruz Bay*

ST JOHN
Trip Builder

Two-thirds of St John is a protected national park, with gnarled trees and spiky cacti spilling over its edges. There are no airports or cruise-ship docks, and the usual Caribbean resorts are few and far between. It's blissfully low-key compared to its island neighbors.

Practicalities

ARRIVING

Most visitors arrive at the **Cruz Bay Ferry Dock** on regular boats from Red Hook in St Thomas. Less-frequent ferries arrive from Charlotte Amalie and the BVI. There is no airport.

FIND YOUR WAY

St John Beach Guide (*stjohn-beachguide.com*) has great tips on picking the right beach for lazing, snorkeling or hiking.

MONEY

There are only three ATMs on island, and they're all in Cruz Bay. Most places accept cards.

WHERE TO STAY

Area	Pros/Cons
Cruz Bay	The ferry landing and main village hosts a hell of a happy hour. It's mostly B&Bs here.
Coral Bay	The sleepy domain of folks who feel as if they're living on the frontier. Only private villas and cottage rentals.
North Shore	Camp – or glamp – in the national park.

EATING & DRINKING

Food on St John has an international flair, with more fusion cuisine than traditional grub. Happy hours in Cruz Bay are legendary as the sun sets over the harbor. Expect everything from sushi to smoothies and protein bowls, plus epic sea views.

Best floating restaurant
Lime Out VI (p86)

Must-try lobster dinner
Morgan's Mango (p86)

GETTING AROUND

Bus Vitran (*dpw.vi.gov*) operates air-con buses over the length of the island via Centerline Rd at least eight times daily. They arrive at Coral Bay about 40 minutes later.

Car St John rentals are all via small, independent companies. Most provide 4WDs and SUVs to handle the rugged terrain. Companies typically have a three- to five-day minimum.

JAN–MAR
It's peak season on St John with dryer, cooler weather.

APR–JUN
The water is at its calmest. Swimmers and snorkelers rejoice.

JUL–SEP
Brave hurricane season to enjoy lower prices. And Carnival!

OCT–DEC
The afternoon showers peter out by Thanksgiving and Christmas.

06 Fall for
'LOVE CITY'

ART | BARS | CULTURE

▬▬ Nicknamed 'Love City,' St John's main town indeed wafts a carefree, spring-break party vibe. Hippies, sea captains, American retirees and reggae worshippers hoist happy-hour drinks in equal measure, and everyone wears a silly grin at their good fortune of being here.

JAMES SCHWABEL/ALAMY

🗺 How to

Getting around Cruz Bay is exceedingly walkable and relatively flat. Most visitors use their own steam to get around.

Top tip Happy hour is a big deal in Cruz Bay and runs roughly from 3pm to 5pm, depending on the place. Expect major discounts and big crowds.

Take a hike Many hikes start right from Cruz Bay, so you can hike in the morning and return to celebrate.

🖼 Bajo El Sol Gallery & Art Bar

Just when you begin to lament the lack of cultural spaces in the USVI you find a place like **Bajo El Sol** (*bajoelsolgallery.com*), which showcases local painters, potters and woodworkers, screens Caribbean documentaries, and runs monthly events such as high-end rum tastings, pop-up dinners and book signings. Also, fine wines and espresso coffees!

02 Looking for paper made out of local donkey poo? Thought so. It's right next door at the **Friends of the Park Store**, along with shelves of ecofriendly wares and sea-glass jewelry. Proceeds go toward conservation.

Virgin Islands National Park

01 Stop in the **Cruz Bay Visitor Center** to get a national park map, read up on local history and plan your onward explorations. Be sure to inquire about ranger-guided tours and programs.

North Shore Rd

03 Head to the high-end Mongoose Junction shopping center for more souvenirs, or beer at the famed **Tap Room**, where St John Brewers makes its sunny, citrusy suds, including mango pale ale.

Cruz Bay

King St

Prince St

Centerline Rd

04 **St John Spice** is your one-stop shop by the ferry dock for bush tea, glass art, hot sauce, rum cake, local spices and other Virgin Islands goods.

Hill St

Enighed Pond

Salt Pond

05 Stroll to nearby Wharfside Village to watch the sunset over Cruz Bay. **La Tapa** is the finest dining option here, specializing in small-plate Spanish-fusion cuisine.

Turner Bay

Southside Rd

07
Hikes in Virgin Islands
NATIONAL PARK

HIKING | BIRDING | RUINS

Virgin Islands National Park covers two-thirds of St John, plus 5650 acres underwater. It's a tremendous resource, offering miles of shoreline, pristine reefs and 26 hiking trails. Many leave right from Cruz Bay, and there are routes for all ages and abilities.

JO CREBBIN/SHUTTERSTOCK

🗺 How to

Getting around The park is best explored on foot, though you may need a transfer to certain trailheads. The cross-island bus **Vitran** *(dpw.vi.gov)* is a great resource for those without a car.

When to go High season (December–March) offers the coolest, driest weather, making it the most ideal for hiking.

Guides The National Park Service (NPS) offers guided hikes and ranger-led programming. Check schedules at the Cruz Bay Visitor Center.

KELLY VANDELLEN/SHUTTERSTOCK

Getting Oriented

The **Cruz Bay Visitor Center** sits on the dock across from the Mongoose Junction shopping arcade and is an essential first stop to obtain intel on hiking, birdwatching, petroglyph sites and ranger-led activities.

Preview trails and download a map at the park website *(nps.gov/viis)*. The **Friends of the Park Store** *(friendsvinp.org/shop)*, next to the visitor center, sells a terrific, more detailed map. Any reasonably fit hiker should be able to walk the park's trails safely without a guide. If you prefer guided jaunts, the park sponsors several free ones, including birding expeditions and shore hikes.

VALERIE JOHNSON/SHUTTERSTOCK

Hiking from Cruz Bay

Some wonderful hikes leave right from the visitor center, including the popular **Lind**

⚠ The Death Apple

Several beaches on St John feature the manchineel plant, which produces a small, green, apple-like fruit. It may be tempting in this tropical Eden to touch or consume it. Don't! Locals call this the 'death apple tree' for good reason, as it's one of the most toxic plants on Earth.

Top left View of Trunk Bay (p81)
Left Lind Point Trail **Above** National park welcome sign

Point Trail, which moseys for 1.1 miles through cactus and dry forest, past the occasional donkey and bananaquit, to **Honeymoon Beach**. A 0.4-mile upper track goes to Lind Battery, once a British gun emplacement, 160ft above the sea. The lower track goes directly to the beach. Alternatively, the **Caneel Hill Trail** leads from the visitor center to a lovely overlook of Cruz Bay about a mile away.

Accessible & Family-Friendly Walks

Families with small children will find several great short hikes within the park. Heading east, the first you come across is the 0.5-mile nature loop at **Cinnamon Bay**, which lies right next to the historic Cinnamon Bay Sugar Plantation. Cinnamon Bay is also the site of the park's only authorized campground, the **Cinnamon Bay Beach & Campground** (*cinnamonbayvi.com*), which has both bare sites and more luxurious 'eco-tents' or cottages.

⛺ Sleep Inside the Park

Aficionados of primitive campsites may find the two restaurants, four bathhouses and well-stocked general store at Cinnamon Bay absolutely luxe; however, there's no disputing the convenience of this campground. Tent rentals are available on-site, and the campground even offers upgrades with actual beds. Campsites come equipped with a grill; however, a food truck and outdoor dining at Rain Tree Cafe mean visitors won't have to work hard for a meal. Kayak, stand-up paddleboard (SUP) and snorkel gear rentals also make enjoying the bay itself a breeze. Solid concrete cottages are also available for those who need a few more creature comforts.

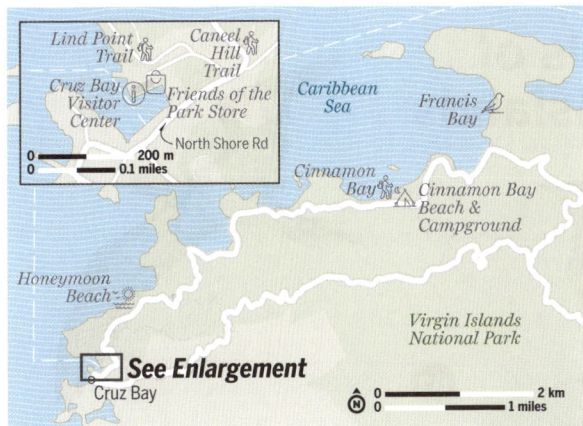

See Enlargement
Cruz Bay

Left Cinnamon Bay **Below** Wild goat

Further along at **Francis Bay** is a lovely salt pond and dry tropical forest, which lies next to the ruins of the Francis Bay Estate House. This is the best spot on St John for birdwatching, with thrashers, stilts, cuckoos, flycatchers and moorhens all frequent visitors. The lower portion of Francis Bay's 0.7-mile loop trail is an accessible boardwalk; it continues into the mangroves to two viewing platforms.

Park Wildlife

Whether you're camping, hiking or driving on St John, it won't be long before you have a close encounter with the island's odd menagerie of feral animals. Hundreds of goats, donkeys, pigs and cats roam the island, descendants of domestic animals abandoned to the jungle eons ago. White-tailed deer and mongooses are two other introduced species that multiplied in unexpected numbers.

The donkeys are the big attention-grabbers. Often, you'll see them on Centerline Rd, where they'll come right up to your car and stick their snouts in any open window. Do not tempt the animals by offering them food or leaving garbage where they can get at it. And do not approach them for photos. While most have a live-and-let-live attitude and don't mind your stepping around them on the trails, they are all capable of aggression if provoked.

The Animals of the Virgin Islands

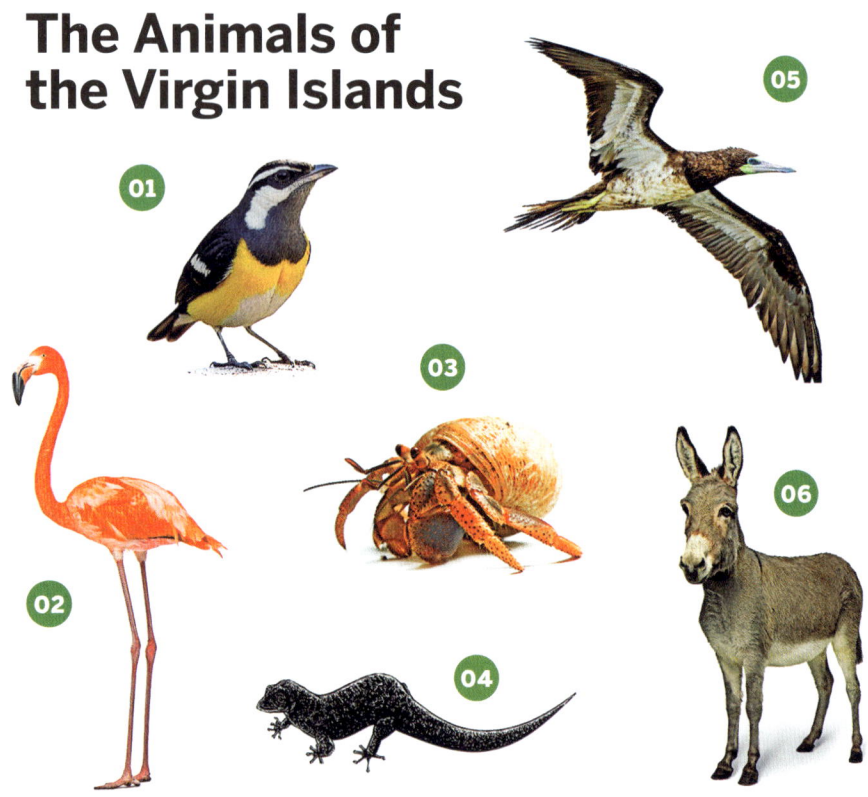

01 Bananaquit
It's the official bird of the USVI and it loves to hang around humans, occasionally stealing fruits and sweets.

02 American Flamingo
These flamboyant waders live in saline lagoons, mudflats and brackish coastal areas, particularly on the island of Anegada.

03 Caribbean Hermit Crab
Also known as soldier crabs, they live inland but migrate to the sea en masse each summer to release their eggs.

04 Virgin Islands Dwarf Sphaero
It's the size of a US dime and is one of the smallest terrestrial vertebrates on Earth, only found in the BVI.

05 Brown Booby
This sleek seabird has a striking blue beak to match its chalky blue legs. It's primarily found in remote offshore islands and cliffs.

06 Donkey
The Danes brought donkeys to St John to haul goods. Now, their feral offspring are island icons, emblazoned on T-shirts and hats.

07 Virgin Islands Coqui

This endemic tree frog is often found hanging out in showers and toilet tanks when it's not hopping around the forest.

08 St Croix Ground Lizard

Endangered and only found on St Croix, male lizards have brilliant blue markings on their light brown bodies.

09 Virgin Islands Tree Boa

This extremely rare and endangered snake can grow over 3ft long. It's nonvenomous and does its hunting at night.

10 Green Iguana

These large lizards love to slink across coastal treetops, but have poor balance and frequently fall. Thankfully, they're great swimmers!

11 Greater Bulldog Bat

Bats like this one are the only native land mammals in the Virgin Islands; there are seven species in total.

12 Mongoose

Introduced from India to control rats, mongooses have, themselves, become a plague, eradicating many native species.

08

Hiking the
REEF BAY TRAIL

HIKING | RUINS | PETROGLYPHS

The Reef Bay Trail deserves its reputation as the premier hike within Virgin Islands National Park. Not only do you explore some spectacular tropical forests, you also dive into the history of St John, from its original Taíno inhabitants to its colonial-era plantations run on the trafficking of enslaved human beings. Though moderately difficult, guided hikes make it a mostly downhill journey.

KELLY VANDELLEN/SHUTTERSTOCK

📷 **How to**

Getting around Ranger-led hikes take care of all logistics. Self-hikers should check bus schedules or arrange transfers.

Wear hiking shoes The trail is in a remote location over uneven and rocky terrain that can be slippery when wet. Sandals won't cut it.

Bring a bathing suit Reef Bay is great for swimming or snorkeling, so you'll want to pack a swimsuit to change into at the end.

KELLY VANDELLEN/SHUTTERSTOCK

JONATHAN A MAUER/SHUTTERSTOCK

Far left top On the Reef Bay Trail
Far left bottom Petroglyph
Left Sugar mill

The Reef Bay Trail is a 3-mile downhill trek to the swimming beach and sugar mill ruins at Reef Bay via the oldest and tallest trees on the island. The trailhead lies on Centerline Rd about 5 miles east of Cruz Bay. A well-marked detour about halfway down takes you to ancient rock art left by the pre-Columbian Taíno people. Look for the swirling petroglyphs at the base of a small waterfall.

Once at Reef Bay, you can decide whether you wish to turn around and retrace your steps, or turn the hike into a larger adventure. Options for the latter include returning to Centerline Rd via the 2.5-mile **L'Esperance Trail**, an old Danish road passing the L'Esperance, Seiban and Mollendahl plantation ruins. Or, for an even greater challenge, you could head back to the Reef Bay Estate Great House Ruins and divert east on the 4-mile **Lameshur Bay Trail**. This ends at a road continuing onward another 1.5 miles to Salt Pond (the end of the bus line).

Reef Bay is the most popular ranger-led walk. Not only will park guides accompany you through the tropical forests, explaining the petroglyphs and plantation ruins in detail; they'll also take you back to Cruz Bay by boat (hence the US$110 fee), making it a largely downhill, one-way hike. It's very popular, and the park recommends reserving at least two weeks ahead. Departure is from the park visitor center.

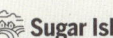 **Sugar Island**

The **Annaberg Plantation** near Leinster Bay (a 30-minute drive from Cruz Bay) is home to the most intact sugar-mill ruins in the Virgin Islands. A 30-minute self-directed walking tour leads you through the 18th-century enslaved people's quarters, village, windmill, rum still and dungeon. Informational plaques along the way offer key insights on the site's human and natural history. There are occasional cultural demonstrations here ranging from basket-weaving to baking traditional 'dumb bread' (a dense, unleavened loaf typical of the Virgin Islands).

A Brief History of the USVI

THE USVI'S LONG ROAD TO BECOMING AN AMERICAN TERRITORY

How did the US end up raising its flag above a string of Caribbean islands? The answer is, well, complicated. To get a better understanding, it's best to go back to the very beginning – before the colonies and slave trade – to when these islands were occupied by their original inhabitants.

DONDRE RICHARDS/SHUTTERSTOCK

Humans have lived here from as early as 2000 BCE. The Taínos ruled the roost for a while, but the ruthless, seafaring Caribs eventually wiped them out. Around this time, during his second trip to the Caribbean, Christopher Columbus sailed up to St Croix's Salt River Bay. It was 1493, and he gave the islands their enduring name: Santa Ursula y Las Once Mil Vírgenes, in honor of a legendary 4th-century princess and her 11,000 maidens. Mapmakers soon shortened the mouthful to 'The Virgins.'

The islands remained under Spanish control until the English defeated the Spanish Armada in 1588. England, France and Denmark were quick to issue 'letters of marque,' which allowed privateers the right to claim territory and protect their claims. One king's privateer became every other king's pirate. Blackbeard (Edward Teach) operated in the Virgin Islands before 1720, along with a collection of other rascals.

The Danes and the English bickered over the islands, while each built vast sugar and tobacco plantations. The English held colonies on islands east of St John, while the Danes held St Thomas to the west. St John remained disputed territory. Finally, in 1717 the Danes sent a small but determined band of soldiers to St John and drove the British out. The Narrows, between St John and Tortola in the British Virgin Islands, became the border that has divided the western (first Danish, now US) Virgins from the British Virgins for nearly three centuries.

Plantation Slavery & its Aftermath

The West Indies grew rich producing sugar and cotton for Europe. In pursuit of profits, the Danish West India and

Left Salt River Bay National Historic Park (p105) **Center** Annaberg Sugar Plantation (p77) **Right** US and USVI flags

Guinea Company declared St Thomas a free port in 1724, and purchased St Croix from the French in 1733. By the end of the century the number of enslaved Africans on the islands exceeded 40,000.

Harsh living conditions and oppressive laws drove enslaved people to revolt. Meanwhile, sugar production in Europe and American tariffs on foreign sugar cut into the islands' profits. The deteriorating economy put everyone in a foul mood. Something had to give and it finally did in 1848, when Afro-Caribbeans on St Croix forced a legal end to slavery. However, they remained in economic bondage. Life on the islands was dismal. A series of labor revolts left the plantation infrastructure in ruins.

> The USA paid the Danes US$25 million in gold for the islands in 1917.

The Islands Change Hands

The USA, realizing the strategic value of the islands, negotiated with Denmark to buy its territories. The deal was almost done in 1867, but the US Congress balked at paying US$7.5 million (more than the US$7.2 million it had just paid for Alaska). As WWI began in Europe, the USA grew concerned that German armies might invade Denmark and claim the Danish West Indies. Finally, the USA paid the Danes US$25 million in gold for the islands in 1917.

Ever since, the islands have been a territory of the USA and, as such, have an elected, nonvoting representative to the US House of Representatives. All citizens of the USVI are US citizens (and have been since 1927), with all the rights that entails, except one: they cannot vote in presidential elections.

Who are the Virgin Islanders?

The USVI wears a veneer of mainstream American life, but West Indian culture is a strong and respected presence. Since 1960 the population of the USVI has nearly quadrupled, although current growth has plateaued.

Economic opportunities draw immigrants from other parts of the West Indies, along with US mainlanders who come to escape the busyness of American life. According to recent census data, 71% of the population is Black, 13% is white and the rest is a mix. About half the population was born in the USVI; another third hail from Latin America or elsewhere in the Caribbean; and about 16% were born in the USA.

09
Beach-Hop the
NORTH SHORE

SWIM | SUNBATHE | KAYAK

Life's a beach on the North Shore, where the national park's main attractions lie, including its most popular patches of sand. Other than sunbathing, snorkeling is the main event here, and a couple of the larger strands rent gear on-site. This is also a prime spot for kayaking or paddleboarding in tranquil protected bays.

🗺 How to

When to go Most beaches have small parking lots, so those with rental cars will want to arrive early.

Getting there The Vitran bus does not travel along North Shore Rd. You'll need to arrange transfers with safari buses in Cruz Bay.

Fees Most beaches on the North Shore are free, with the exception being Trunk Bay, which charges an 'expanded amenity fee' of US$5 per person.

ROBERT COLONNA/SHUTTERSTOCK

Far left top Trunk Bay
Far left bottom Maho Bay
Left Hawksnest Bay

There are no bad beaches on the North Shore, which boasts a string of back-to-back show-stoppers. The first on the road out of town is **Hawksnest Bay**, which lies in a deep cove between hills. It's a tad thin and remains peaceful as a result. Amenities include a bathroom, picnic shelter and barbecue grills. Quieter still is **Jumbie Bay**, whose secluded Gibney Beach is wrapped up in local lore involving the Oppenheimer family (former residents). Look for the parking lot on North Shore Rd that holds seven cars.

Next are a string of wide, popular beaches starting with the gently arching **Trunk Bay**, which boasts showers, picnic facilities, water-sports rentals, dining options and the kind of crowds you won't find anywhere else. Neighboring **Cinnamon Bay** has the same level of facilities but no cruise-ship visitors from St Thomas. **Maho Bay**, further along, is even better for those who want smaller crowds, plus a high chance of sea turtles and stingrays.

Prefer to paddle the coast? **Arawak Expeditions** (arawak exp.com) offers North Shore kayak-and-snorkel tours right from Cruz Bay, which can last either three or six hours. Outings traverse the typically exciting waters of Sir Francis Drake Channel while taking visitors past the national park's Honeymoon Beach and into Caneel Bay, where the ruins of St John's most prominent Rockefeller-era retreat rest much as they did after hurricanes Irma and Maria passed through in 2017.

☼ Take Wellness Outdoors

The year-round warm climate and steady breeze make St John an ideal place for taking your wellness activities outside. You can stay active while also enjoying the island's natural scenery. One great place for this is **Hurricane Hole**. Grab a stand-up paddleboard, and pack a lunch, sunscreen and plenty of water for a full-day adventure paddle-boarding the calm waters from one creek to the next. The mangrove-lined shore is a magnificent area for snorkeling. Within the forest of the red mangrove roots you'll see a large variety of juvenile fish and turtles along with corals and bright sea anemones.

Recommended by **Thais Taylor**, owner of Solshine Mindful Yoga. @solshinemindfulyoga

10

Hiking & Snorkeling Near
CORAL BAY

HIKING | SNORKELING | NIGHTLIFE

St John's second town Coral Bay is a slow-poke frontier outpost with a handful of low-key restaurants and bars. Though it's just 8 miles from Cruz Bay, it feels a world away, making it a great base for wild hikes to solitary beaches in the East End or Salt Pond, which are ideal for snorkeling.

🗺 How to

When to go Want to escape the tourist trail of Cruz Bay? Spend an evening with the locals at the bars of Coral Bay.

Getting there Vitran (*dpw.vi.gov*) buses connect Cruz Bay with Coral Bay and Salt Pond seven times daily. To visit the East End, you need your own wheels.

Hiking tip Fewer tourists hike the trails in this sector; research routes in advance and let someone know where you're going.

Some of St John's best snorkeling is around the offshore **Waterlemon Cay**, where turtles, spotted eagle rays and nurse sharks swim. Be aware that the current can be strong. There are no amenities and usually few people out here. Reaching Waterlemon is part of the fun. Most tourists set off on the 0.8-mile **Leinster Bay Trail**, which starts near the Annaberg Sugar Plantation. Yet, you can also reach it via the 1.8-mile **Johnny Horn Trail** from Coral Bay.

The quick, half-mile **Salt Pond Trail**, further south, takes you to a calm beach with some of St John's finest snorkeling, with great chances for spotting sea turtles in the seagrass and barracudas in the border reefs. But the fun doesn't end there. Two dandy trails take off from the beach's southern end.

🐟 Aquanauts

Between 1969 and 1970, the US government sent groups of 'aquanauts' to live for several weeks in an underwater habitat off the coast of St John. The stated goal of the project was to study the psychological effects of humans working in closed environments. The second mission, led by Sylvia Earle, was a pioneering all-female research team. Little remains of this bizarre, science fiction–like experiment, known as Tektite. A small museum dedicated to the project was destroyed in the 2017 hurricanes, but you can still snorkel into the waters of Great Lameshur Bay to see the Tektite's old foundation pads.

The **Drunk Bay Trail** follows the rim of the inland salt pond to a wild, rocky beach that faces east to the BVI. Waves carry all manner of coral, fishing nets and other flotsam that locals sculpt into eye-popping artworks here; it's 0.6 miles round trip. Meanwhile, the

Ram Head Trail is a moderate climb from Salt Pond Bay over switchbacks to Ram Head promontory, 200ft above the water at St John's southernmost tip, a grandly lonesome and windswept place. It's 2 miles round trip and exposed, so bring sun protection.

Above Leinster Bay

11

A Private Island
EXPERIENCE

BEACHES | SUNTANNING | COCKTAILS

Those who truly want to escape from it all should head 1.5 miles offshore from Cruz Bay to Lovango Cay, the ultimate Robinson Crusoe escape for barefoot luxury at its finest. Most of the island is privately owned; however, the Lovango Resort + Beach Club welcomes guests who want to experience their own slice of paradise for the day.

PICS721/SHUTTERSTOCK

How to

When to go The resort is open mid-December to mid-July.

Getting there Lovango is a 10-minute ferry ride from St John's Cruz Bay; take a private boat or use one of the beach resort's ferries.

Club fees Boats deposit visitors on the doorstep of the resort, where the staff are happy to propel you around the island on golf carts, provided you pay the daily membership fee (from US$150).

PICS721/SHUTTERSTOCK

CDWHEATLEY/GETTY IMAGES

Far left top and bottom Lovango Cay
Left Paddleboarding Lovango Cay

With room prices well above US$1000 per night, **Lovango Resort + Beach Club** (lovangovi.com) may be out of reach for most travelers. Yet, for a fraction of that cost, you can simply rent the lifestyle of the rich and famous for one day, accessing all of the resort's main facilities. The three tiers of daily 'club membership' all include seaside chaise loungers, snorkeling equipment, shower facilities, beach games, food and drink offerings, and a 70ft infinity pool with towel service.

You can dine in one of the two waterfront restaurants, shop at the six boutiques, beef up at the 'gym in the jungle,' or simply lounge by the beach or pool. Sublime snorkeling around the docks next to the beach club is one of the USVI's best-kept secrets.

Lovango Cay – at just 118 acres – is small even by island standards, and there is a great network of trails to help you get out and explore. Hike from the beach club to the island's summit via the **BVI Trail**, which offers sweeping views over Tortola and Jost Van Dyke. Then, travel onward to hidden **Crescent Beach**. During calm seas, Crescent Beach is a fantastic place to go for a swim or snorkel on a seldom accessed reef; it's one of three reefs the resort is actively restoring in an innovative partnership with the University of the Virgin Islands.

⚓ The Legend of Lovango

Lovango Cay derives its name from its colorful history as a haven for brothels in the 18th century. As the story goes, sailors leaving the West Indies would make a pit stop here before setting off to sea. Local legends attribute the name to pirates, who coined the term 'Love and Go Island.' As always in the Caribbean, pirate tales are to be taken with a grain of salt. According to the St John Historical Society, the name may actually come from the title of an African trading post in the Congo. The nearby cays of Congo and Mingo also feature African names, adding credibility to this theory.

Listings

BEST OF THE REST

Caribbean Flavors

Uncle Joe's BBQ $

Locals and visitors alike go wild tearing into the barbecue chicken, ribs and corn on the cob at this open-air restaurant across from the post office. The chef grills the meats outside, perfuming the entire harborfront with tangy goodness.

Miss Lucy's $$

Though Miss Lucy passed away in 2007, her Salt Pond–area restaurant lives on, as famous for its callaloo (a leafy green) and crab soup as for its conch fritters and johnnycakes – all served at the water's edge under the sea-grape trees as the occasional pet goat wanders by.

Morgan's Mango $$$

Take in a view of the harbor while dining on imaginative Caribbean recipes in dishes such as rum-glazed mahi-mahi or Cuban citrus chicken. The owners often bring in live acoustic acts, making Morgan's a good choice for a fun or romantic night out.

The Longboard $$$

Fresh, healthy, veggie- and grain-packed meals make this whitewashed, surf-themed spot stand out from the greasy, deep-fried pack. Enjoy raw fish as poke, ceviche or sushi, or munch on a fully loaded quinoa bowl. Your body will thank you!

Day Drinking in the Sun

Lime Out VI $$

What could be more gratifying than boating into the turquoise sea, docking up to a floating solar-powered restaurant, swimming over to the bar, and noshing on tacos packed with blackened tuna or rum-glazed ribs? Oh, and then there are creative craft cocktails served in reusable adult sippy cups. Make an afternoon of it!

Skinny Legs $$

Salty sailors and East End villa dwellers mix it up at this open-air grill just past the Coral Bay fire station. Overlooking a small boatyard, Skinny Legs' focus isn't the view but the jovial clientele and the lively bar scene. Live music and dancing rock weekend nights.

Maho Crossroads $$

This minimum-footprint pop-up village has a beach shop, a food truck, water sports, cornhole (a lawn game) and colorful picnic chairs, all set amid a papaya grove at Maho Beach. Most folks come to sidle up to the bar and sip painkillers or bushwackers (both local cocktails). Rent your snorkels or paddleboards here, too.

Uncle Joe's BBQ

Guided Sea Adventures

Low Key Watersports

A great dive-training facility with some of the most experienced instructors on the islands. It offers wreck dives to the RMS *Rhone*, as well as night dives and dive packages. It also has speedboat charters for day trips to the Baths or Jost Van Dyke in the BVI.

Cruz Bay Watersports

Located at the Westin Resort, this company goes out for daily snorkel trips around St John with stops at places like Lime Out or Lovango Cay. It also offers sunset cruises and sailing jaunts to the BVI's Baths and Jost Van Dyke.

Solshine Mindful Yoga

Let bubbly SUP and yoga instructor Thais take you into the water for some paddleboard yoga or a ride around Coral Bay Harbor to the Lime Out taco joint. Other tours include a Hurricane Hole paddle or a hike and yoga combo.

Virgin Island Ecotours

This groovy company, which also operates on St Thomas, offers several guided jaunts that include kayaking, snorkeling and/or hiking. Some trips are kid-friendly, some strenuous. Most tours depart from Honeymoon Beach, but a few leave near the national park visitor center.

More History, Please

Peace Hill

Look for the Peace Hill sign as you drive between Hawksnest and Jumbie Bays. Pull into the small parking lot, and if you're willing

ROBERT COLONNA/SHUTTERSTOCK

Peace Hill

to walk 0.1 miles you'll be rewarded with the moody ruins of an old windmill and pretty views out to sea. A *Christ of the Caribbean* statue once crowned the hill, but Hurricane Marilyn in 1995 proved to be the stronger force.

More Coral Bay Activities

St John VI Pottery

This ceramics studio offers Make Pottery in Paradise classes where you can learn to work the wheel. Teachers glaze your work after the fact and ship it to you within two weeks. The studio's wares are also for sale in a small shop.

Carolina Corral

Saddle up a trusty steed for a 1½-hour jaunt on rugged trails to a rocky beach. All the horses are rescue animals.

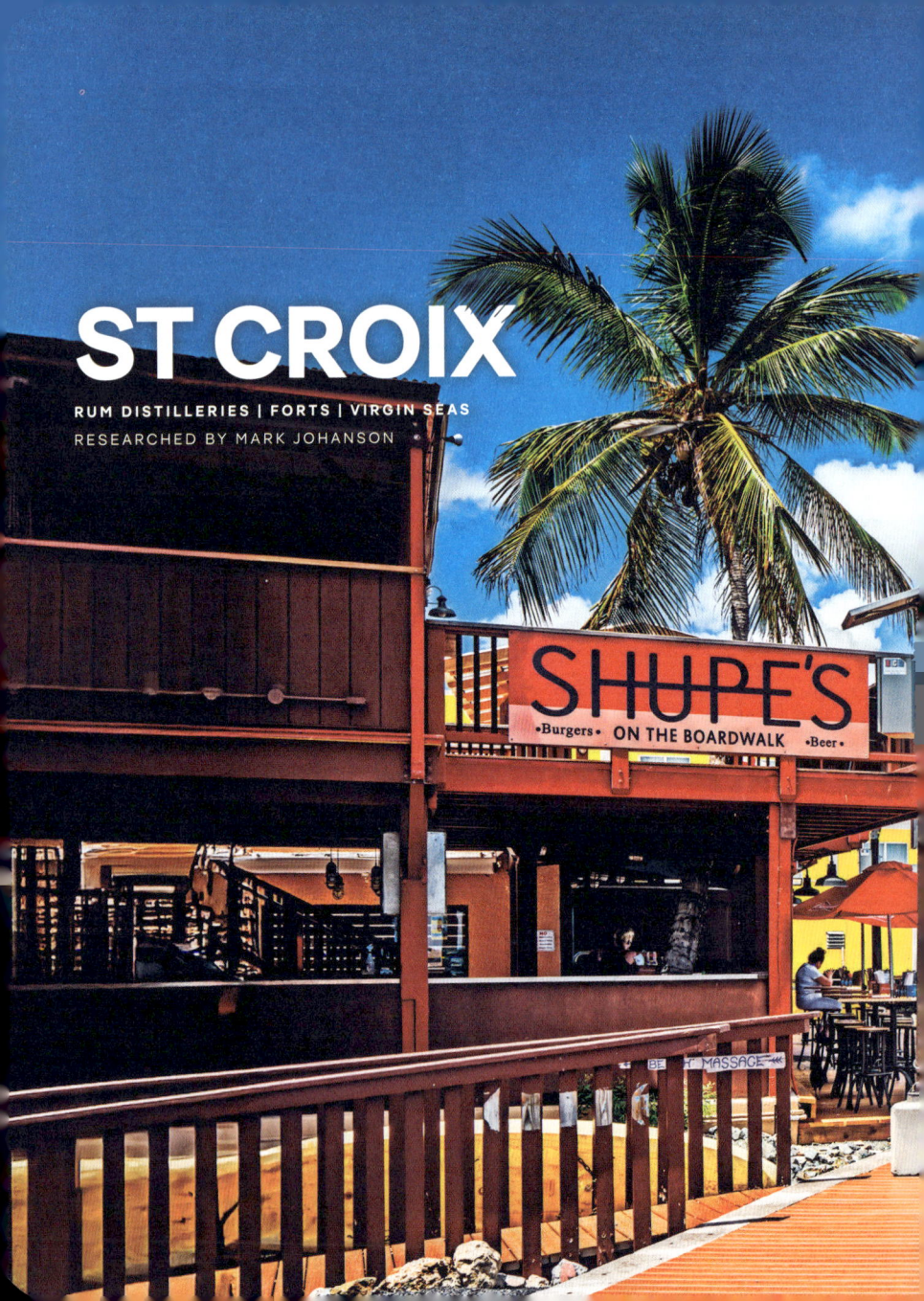

ST CROIX

RUM DISTILLERIES | FORTS | VIRGIN SEAS

RESEARCHED BY MARK JOHANSON

▶ **Trip Builder** (p90)

▶ **Practicalities** (p91)

▶ **Stroll Through History in Christiansted** (p92)

▶ **Soak Up the Flavors** (p94)

▶ **The 'Founding Father' Raised in Christiansted** (p96)

▶ **Escape to Buck Island** (p98)

▶ **The Easternmost Point in the USA** (p102)

▶ **Roam the Wild North Shore** (p104)

▶ **Swim in Wild Ocean Pools** (p106)

▶ **Explore Historic Frederiksted** (p108)

▶ **How Virgin are the Islands?** (p110)

▶ **Listings** (p112)

Dive the world-famous **Cane Bay Wall** (p101).
🚗 30 min from Christiansted

Kayak atop the bioluminescent waters of **Salt River Bay** (p104).
🚗 20 min from Christiansted

Take a snorkeling trip to the **Buck Island Reef National Monument** (p98).
⛴ 40 min from Christiansted

Caribbean Sea

Buck Island

△ *Mt Eagle*

Christiansted

○ Frederiksted

Search for sea turtles at the **Jack and Isaac Bay Preserve** (p102).
🚗 🚶 1 hr from Christiansted

Taste the golden spirit of the USVI at the **Cruzan Rum Distillery** (p95).
🚗 30 min from Christiansted

Stroll through pastel-colored colonial buildings in historic **Christiansted** (p92; pictured).
🚗 25 min from Henry E Rohlsen Airport

ST CROIX
Trip Builder

St Croix is the largest Virgin with an exceptional topography spanning mountains, 'rainforest' and fertile plains that, once upon a time, earned it the nickname 'Garden of the Antilles.' Today the island is known for its scuba diving, rum-making, marine sanctuary and 18th-century forts.

Practicalities

ARRIVING

St Croix's **Henry E Rohlsen Airport** handles flights from the US, some connecting via San Juan, Puerto Rico, or St Thomas. Seaborne Airlines flies seaplanes between St Thomas and Christiansted's downtown harbor.

FIND YOUR WAY

The highways on St Croix are the best in the USVI – you can even speed up to 55mph on some stretches!

MONEY

Credit cards and ATMs are commonplace here, so no need to carry around much cash.

WHERE TO STAY

Area	Pros/Cons
Christiansted	Conveniently located downtown, walkable to bars, shops and restaurants. Slightly older and more traditional.
Frederiksted	Low-key, more alternative seafront stays. Top choice for LGBTIQ+ travelers and their allies.
North Shore	More casual than glamorous; there are cute B&Bs ideal for divers and beach strollers.

EATING & DRINKING

St Croix is the chain's finest culinary destination and the only Virgin Island with some real agricultural lands. Rum is big business here with not one but two major distilleries. There are also two craft breweries, which infuse local fruits into their ales.

Best rum tasting
Cruzan Rum Distillery (p95; pictured)

Must-try beer
Leatherback Brewing Company (p95)

GETTING AROUND

Ferry QE IV Ferry runs twice-daily ferries (2½ hours) between Gallows Bay on St Croix and Blyden Terminal on St Thomas.

Bus Vitran buses travel along Centerline Rd between Christiansted and Frederiksted roughly every two hours in daylight.

Car Rentals start at about US$55 per day. Hire at the airport or seaplane dock.

ST CROIX FIND YOUR FEET

JAN–MAR
St Croix starts the year with a blow-out Carnival (and high season).

APR–JUN
Shoulder season means lower prices but no threat of hurricanes.

JUL–SEP
It's hot and sleepy and a great time to commune with locals.

OCT–DEC
Conch season begins, so the mollusks are widely available.

Stroll Through History in
CHRISTIANSTED

ST CROIX EXPERIENCES

HARBOR | HISTORY | ARCHITECTURE

Located 40 miles south of Charlotte Amalie and the distant din of St Thomas, St Croix can feel positively quiet by contrast; Christiansted is the lone exception. This town of just 3000 evokes a melancholy hint of the past, harboring stories of colonization and liberation that are best absorbed bit by bit on a historic walk.

E W Y MEDIA/SHUTTERSTOCK

🗺 How to

When to go No need to worry about crowds at these historic sites unless there's a cruise ship in port over in Frederiksted. You'll often have them all to yourself.

Getting around
Everything in historic Christiansted is within easy walking distance on flat roads.

Costs The fort belongs to the National Park Service (NPS), so you'll need to pay a US$10 park entry fee.

E W Y MEDIA/SHUTTERSTOCK

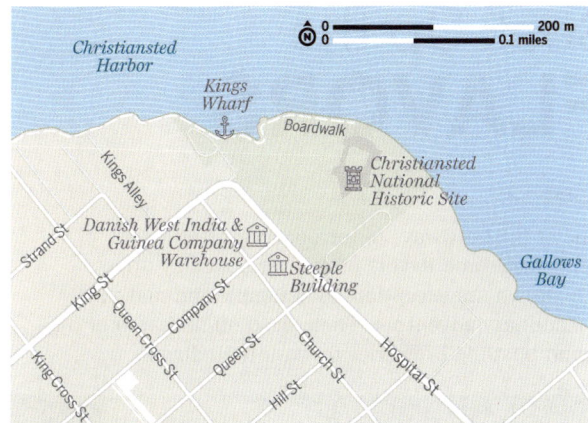

Far left top Christiansted National Historic Site **Far left bottom** Steeple Building

The **Christiansted National Historic Site** (*nps.gov/chri/index.htm*) holds many key structures. The most impressive is Fort Christiansvaern, a four-point citadel occupying the mustard-yellow buildings on the town's eastern edge. Built out of Danish bricks (brought over as ships' ballast) in 1749, the fort guarded against pirate onslaughts, hurricanes and slave revolts. Cannons on the ramparts, an echoey, claustrophobic dungeon, and latrines with top-notch sea views await inside.

Across the street from the fort lies the **Danish West India & Guinea Company Warehouse**. This three-story Danish colonial building began life in 1749 as the headquarters and warehouse for the Danish West India and Guinea Company. The central courtyard was the site of one of the West Indies' most active slave markets until the abolition of the slave trade in 1848. The building is privately owned, so you can't go inside. The white building with the Georgian steeple next door was St Croix' first house of worship. Lutherans erected the edifice of the **Steeple Building** between 1750 and 1753, adding the tower four decades later.

The greater fort complex abuts **Kings Wharf**, the commercial docks where, for more than 250 years, ships landed with enslaved people and set off with sugar or molasses. Today the wharf is fronted by a boardwalk full of restaurants, dive shops and bars. After a leisurely walk along the seaside, dip into the historic archways and ramparts for an eye-opening, educational experience.

☵ Set Sail!

Three masts, seven sails and 137ft of wooden decks play host to travelers in Christiansted from November to March, when the **World Ocean School** (*worldoceanschool.org/st-croix-sails*) offers two-hour sunset cruises aboard the *Denis Sullivan*, a replica of a Great Lakes schooner. The best part: sailings help support World Ocean School's ongoing work with elementary and high school students on St Croix, where it hosts lectures, labs and STEM classes. Guests on the evening trips can help hoist the sails or simply settle in for sublime views beside the cash bar, where you can order a rum and Coke.

Soak Up the
FLAVORS

RUM | GASTRONOMY | CULTURE

▬▬▬ A walking tour is one of the best ways to introduce yourself to Christiansted while exploring areas and flavors often overlooked by other travelers. The streets of downtown are exceptionally walkable and make a picturesque backdrop for a culinary adventure. Then, head off in search of the island's famed distilleries and bustling breweries to wash it all down.

EA GIVEN/SHUTTERSTOCK

🗺 How to

Get around A taxi from Christiansted out to the breweries or distilleries should cost about US$24. Otherwise, it's best to rent a car.

Booking Some of the distilleries ask you to book your tour in advance.

Breweries don't require bookings, and serve food alongside beer.

Best time to visit The Taste of St Croix festival unites more than 40 restaurants, caterers and farms for one epic night of fine dining each April.

KERRICK JAMES/ALAMY

THE IMAGE PARTY/SHUTTERSTOCK

Far left top Waterfront restaurants
Far left bottom Cruzan rum
Left Jerk chicken

Locally owned restaurants, specialty food shops and St Croix's signature rum take center stage with chef and self-described foodie Anquanette Gaspard's Taste of the Twin City Food Tour, from **Virgin Islands Food Tours** (vifoodtours.com). These three-hour tours bring visitors to six savory locations in downtown Christiansted. Dip into fascinating history and little-known facts about St Croix as Anquanette guides you through plates of traditional fare, such as jerk chicken and callaloo (spicy soup with okra, meats and greens), as well as the avant-garde flavors of Caribbean fusion that incorporate Latin and Trinidadian dishes.

Spirits enthusiasts should then take the road out to the airport to a string of distilleries – none more famous than the **Captain Morgan Rum Distillery** (captainmorganvisitorcenter.com), whose tours span multimedia films, information panels and, of course, samples of the Captain's happy juice. More authentic to the USVI is the nearby **Cruzan Rum Distillery** (cruzanrum.com), whose tours educate visitors on how to craft the islands' popular elixir. Journey through the oak-barrel-stacked warehouses, with their aroma of gingerbread (from the molasses and yeast), before sipping plenty of the good stuff. The Nelthropp family, Cruzan Rum's owners, have been perfecting the recipes since 1760.

The Caribbean may not be known for vodka, but **Sion Farm Distillery** (sionfarmdistillery.com) hopes to change that with its Mutiny Vodka, which is distilled from island breadfruits. Visitors can tour the facility – an old dairy factory – and sample the spirit, which has hints of melon, citrus and green banana.

Craft Cruzan Ales

More of a beer fan? **Brew STX** (brewstx.com) is on the Christiansted boardwalk, overlooking yachts bobbing in the sea, and is primo for sampling the small-batch suds cooked up steps away from the taps. These include blondes, stouts, citrus ales and even sours. Out by the airport is the **Leatherback Brewing Company** (leatherbackbrewing.com), where you can sidle up to the indoor-outdoor bar and order one of the six home-brewed beers on tap, including the signature trio: Island Life lager, Reef Life IPA and Beach Life blonde ale. There are also sandwiches, snacks and a popular Sunday brunch.

The 'Founding Father' Raised in Christiansted

HAMILTON – YES, *THAT* HAMILTON – GREW UP ON ST CROIX

For 250 years, no one cared much about Alexander Hamilton, the guy on the US$10 bill. That he came of age in Christiansted elicited little more than passing yawns. Then, Lin-Manuel Miranda penned the musical *Hamilton*, which hit the stage in 2015 and became a Broadway smash.

CFG1978/SHUTTERSTOCK

Hamilton won Pulitzer, Tony and Grammy awards for telling the story of this historic figure in an innovative way via hip-hop tunes. Now, visitors want to know more about how one of America's Founding Fathers spent his formative years in the Caribbean.

Who was Hamilton?

Hamilton was actually born on the neighboring island of Nevis in 1755, but he lived from age seven to 17 in Christiansted. His was a hard-knock life – born illegitimately, orphaned by age 12, impoverished – but he worked hard and impressed the local merchants, who sent him to school in New York, where he flourished and became a major voice during the Revolutionary War. George Washington appointed him as the architect of the new country's economic policies. In 1789 Hamilton became the first secretary of the treasury – which is what earned him the honor of being on the US currency. He died infamously in 1804 in a duel with rival politician Aaron Burr, who was the vice president at the time.

Hamilton's Christiansted

The entrance at Fort Christiansvaern has brochures about Hamilton's time on St Croix, including a self-guided walking tour of the places he frequented. Alas, most of the buildings from the era have been destroyed, so you'll have to use your imagination to see where young Alex lived and worked (at a store selling plantation supplies). One place that does still exist: the cell at Fort Christiansvaern where

Left US$10 bills **Center** Fort Christiansvaern cell **Right** Fort Christiansvaern

EWY MEDIA/SHUTTERSTOCK

EWY MEDIA/SHUTTERSTOCK

his mom, Rachel Lavien, was imprisoned for leaving her first husband, a man of ill repute who was 16 years her senior.

Lavien later died on St Croix in 1768 of yellow fever, which had a severe emotional impact on the bereaved child, whose father had abandoned him. Young Alex and his stepbrother were adopted by a cousin, Peter Lytton. But tragedy was, once again, lurking around the corner. Lytton committed suicide just 17 months later. Hamilton bounced around the Caribbean in the ensuing years until, in 1772, he left for good. The rest, of course, is history.

> Hamilton bounced around the Caribbean ... until, in 1772, he left for good. The rest, of course, is history.

Hamilton Tours

The **Eyes of Hamilton Tour** (eyesofhamiltontours.com) is a two-hour trip around Christiansted guided by local historian Wayne Nichols, who dresses up in period costume. Nichols prides himself on historical accuracy, offering an entertaining trip rich in storytelling that evokes the look and feel of 18th-century St Croix.

Another fun way to explore Hamilton's legacy is to go on a **geocache** (geocaching.com) tour around Christiansted, where you'll learn about his life here and how his experience with commerce at the shop downtown laid the foundation for his future work in the US government. Finding the cache involves visiting six historic sites, each of which offers a number used to complete the coordinates for the final location.

📖 The Plantation Era

Head to the **Estate Whim Museum** (stcroixlandmarks.org) for more historical context into St Croix. Only 12 of the Whim Plantation's original 150 acres survive at the museum, but the grounds thoroughly evoke the colonial days when sugarcane ruled the island. Visitors can wander past the crumbling stone windmill, the stately Great House and the humble laborer's quarters, stewing on what life was like for both the rich white landowners and the Black enslaved people. Expect an honest and unflinching look at the realities of 19th-century St Croix – and be sure to check out the library, archives and rotating exhibitions.

Escape to
BUCK ISLAND

SNORKELING | DIVING | HIKING

One of the Caribbean's most marvelous marine ecosystems beckons adventurous travelers to Buck Island, a remote outpost a mile and a half off the coast of St Croix. This is the best spot in the USVI to snorkel and is great for novice divers, too.

CHRIS ALLAN/SHUTTERSTOCK

🗺 How to

Getting here & around
Big Beard's Adventure Tours and Caribbean Sea Adventures operate guided tours and sunset cruises to Buck Island from Christiansted. The journey takes about 45 minutes.

Boat permits Sailors on hired boats will need an anchoring permit from the NPS to moor up.

How long to stay Both half-day and full-day tours are available. It's worth spending a whole day to enjoy both land and sea activities.

DON HEBERT/GETTY IMAGES

ST CROIX EXPERIENCES

Arriving on Buck Island

Buck Island Reef National Monument (*nps. gov/buis*), one of just two submerged national monuments in the US, is a nursery for lemon sharks, a safe haven for seabirds and the home of important biological research on Caribbean ecosystems. The topside is walkable, so be sure to take the short, 45-minute cross-island hiking trail to **Diedrichs Point** and the breezy walk back to **West Beach**. Both spots have picnic tables, charcoal grills and vault toilets. There's a lovely observation deck halfway between in the island's interior.

Turtle Beach, in the island's southwest corner, offers expansive views of St Croix along with a powdery, white-sand surface that often lands it on lists of the world's most beautiful beaches. A quick dip into the

MALACHI JACOBS/SHUTTERSTOCK

🗺 How Many Buck-ing Islands?

There's not one, not two, but rather three Buck Islands in the Virgin Islands! One off the south coast of St Thomas is known primarily for its Danish-built lighthouse and offshore shipwreck. The other near Tortola was the site of the first airstrip in the BVI, but today holds a luxury resort.

Top left Buck Island beach **Left** Snorkeling excursion, Buck Island **Above** View of Buck Island

aquamarine waters helps explain the name, as you encounter green turtles munching on dense meadows of seagrass.

Snorkeling & Diving the Reef

Two-thirds of this uninhabited island is surrounded by a barrier reef, which means most of the recreational opportunities are below the water. Snorkeling is the most popular, and the **Buck Island Reef Underwater Trail** is easily the star of the show. The trail skirts coral grottoes with a maximum water depth of just 12ft, ensuring excellent visibility. The enormous, branching elkhorn form fortress-like walls, and there are plaques describing marine life. Some 250 fish species can be found here, including colorful tangs, eagle rays and the occasional reef shark.

All tour operators on Buck Island must be licensed by the National Park Service, and most offer snorkel lessons for those less comfortable in the water. Entry-level divers

Best Snorkeling & Diving Outfits

Cane Bay Dive Shop
Recommended outfit located near the Frederiksted pier, though its boats depart from Salt River Marina.

Dive Experience
Owned by master instructor Michelle Pugh, this shop in Christiansted has been around for 40-plus years.

Nep2une Scuba Diving
Specializes in West End wreck dives, Frederiksted Pier dives and night dives.

St Croix Ultimate Bluewater Adventures
An ultraprofessional company that offers dives all over the island.

Big Beard's Adventure Tours
Travel to Buck Island aboard a 42ft catamaran for full-day snorkel trips.

Caribbean Sea Adventures
Half- or full-day Buck Island snorkel tours, some of which include hiking.

Far left Snorkeling, Buck Island
Left Cane Bay Wall
Below Diving at Frederiksted Pier

can also take advantage of the outer reef's shallow 30ft to 45ft dives, which are a perfect introduction to diving via a Discover Scuba experience. There are two designated scuba moorings where you can plunge through haystack formations of elkhorn coral.

Diving Elsewhere in St Croix

If you are a scuba enthusiast worth your sea salt, you'll be spending lots of time underwater in St Croix. It's a diver's mecca thanks to two unique features: one, it's surrounded by a massive barrier reef, so turtles, rays and other sea creatures are prevalent; and, two, a spectacular wall runs along the island's north shore, dropping at a 60-degree slope to a depth of more than 3200ft.

The best dives on the north shore are at **Cane Bay Wall** and **North Star Wall**. The top west-island dives are at the Butler Bay shipwrecks (including the *Suffolk Maid* and *Rosaomaira*) and at **Frederiksted Pier**. While almost all dive operators offer boat dives, many of the most exciting dives, such as Cane Bay, involve beach entries with short swims to the reef.

The Easternmost Point
IN THE USA

BEACHES | TURTLES | HIKING

The scalloped coastline and steep, bone-dry hills of the East End beg for a drive. Navigate East End Rd as it unfurls along the beach-strewn northern shore, rolling all the way to Point Udall for sublime views and hikes to a turtle-inhabited nature preserve.

BENUS C MATHURIN/SHUTTERSTOCK

🐢 Turtle Time

The **Jack and Isaac Bay Preserve**, once slated for residential development, is now managed by the Nature Conservancy (TNC) as part of a sanctuary for green and hawksbill turtles, which are active from July to December. TNC ensures that these endangered turtles can nest onshore, and that their young hatchlings make it safely to sea.

🗺 How to

Getting around Point Udall (pictured) is about 12 miles (30 minutes) east of Christiansted. Renting a car is a must; there's no public transport here.

Bring supplies There are few facilities in this far-off corner of St Croix, so be sure to pack water and some snacks.

Help the turtles Avoid visiting the nature preserve at night during nesting season as lights can cause female turtles to abort nesting or lose egg clutches.

02 Just east of the antenna is a trail leading up to **Goat Mountain**, a 672ft hill offering panoramic views. The trek is 2 miles round trip through flowering Ginger Thomas bushes and prickly cacti.

03 **Point Udall** is the easternmost geographic point in US territory. There's a sundial known as the Millennium Monument here, plus a windy vista from a promontory high above surf-strewn beaches.

01 Geek out at the **Very Long Baseline Array Telescope** (pictured), part of a network of 10 similar observing stations across the US, each with an 80ft radio antenna dish and control building.

04 Hikers will enjoy the steep 20-minute path down from Point Udall to isolated **Isaac Bay**, a nesting area for sea turtles. There's no shade or facilities, but it's a stunning stretch of sand.

05 From the western end of Isaac the trail continues to **Jack Bay**, which is also part of the nature preserve. Nudists sometimes hang out on the beaches here.

Goat Mountain

Point Udall

Caribbean Sea

0 | 500 m
0 | 0.25 miles

FROM TOP: JAE BOOTHE/SHUTTERSTOCK, SANDRA FOYT/SHUTTERSTOCK

16

Roam the Wild
NORTH SHORE

HISTORY | SEALIFE | BIOLUMINESCENCE

Bioluminescent bays, Christopher Columbus' landing pad and hot dive sites all await visitors along the North Shore, which is dotted in tidal marshes, wild beaches and low-key towns. This is one of the best spots on the island for active travelers.

BENJAMIN VELAZQUEZ/GETTY IMAGES

🗺 How to

Getting around Buses do not ply the North Shore Rd, so you'll want your own wheels.

When to go January and February are the best months to enjoy the bioluminescence; moon-free nights are a good bet the rest of the year.

Kayaking Virgin Kayak Tours (*virginkayaktours.com*) offers pedal-driven kayaks that are easy for novices to maneuver. Tour the mangrove estuary by day, and the bioluminescent bay at night.

🐟 Deep-Sea Fishing

Deep-sea fishing starts just a few miles offshore. St Croix-born Captain Ryan at **Lioness Sportfishing** (*fishinginstcroix. com*) honed his skills as a commercial fisherman in Alaska, à la *Deadliest Catch* (US reality TV series). With 30 years of experience, he'll get you on the fish.

 Recommended by **Cindy Clearwater**, curator of @MyStCroix. *mystcroix.vi*

05 Kayaking at night through the glowing waters of **Bio Bay** is a St Croix highlight. These bluish-green 'living lights' are actually dinoflagellates, a marine plankton that occurs here in high concentrations.

Caribbean Sea

01 Nine miles west of Christiansted, **Cane Bay** (pictured left) is deservedly popular as it provides easy access to dive sites and forested hills. The long beach has several restaurants great for a seaside lunch.

03 **Salt River Bay National Historic Park** (pictured below) holds prehistoric archaeological ruins and is the only documented place where Christopher Columbus landed on US soil. Don't expect bells and whistles; this NPS site remains largely undeveloped.

04 The 700 acres surrounding the **Salt River Estuary** form an ecological reserve filled with mangroves, egrets and a submarine canyon. Several ecotourism operators run outings from here.

Mt Eagle

Salt River

02 The main reason you come to Cane Bay is to explore **the Wall**, a 3200ft abyss created by the Puerto Rico Trench. This wonderland for deep dives is a quick swim offshore.

DANITA DELIMONT/SHUTTERSTOCK

Swim in Wild
OCEAN POOLS

HIKING | SWIMMING | ADVENTURE

The Annaly Bay Tide Pools are among St Croix's most remote attractions. Carved into the rock walls of the island's northwestern coast, they can only be accessed on foot or by 4WD vehicle. These Jacuzzi-sized baths, reaching depths of up to 5ft, offer a wild experience for those seeking more rugged adventures.

BENIUS C MATHURIN/SHUTTERSTOCK

🗺 How to

When to go It's safest to visit the tide pools during low tide, as wavy conditions or rising tides can be hazardous.

Where to park Parking at Carambola Beach Resort is reserved for guests, but there's nearby parking for accessing the tide pool trail.

What to bring There are no facilities here, so be sure to bring water, snacks and supplies. Also, don't hike in sandals; closed-toe shoes are essential.

ERIN6643/SHUTTERSTOCK

DANITA DELIMONT/SHUTTERSTOCK

Far left top and bottom Annaly Bay Tide Pools **Left** Carambola Beach Resort

A weathered, wooden sign sits near the tree line on Prosperity Rd just south of the Carambola Beach Resort, marking the start of the 2.5-mile **Trumbull Trail**. The uneven path traverses roots and shallow stream crossings, dipping into valleys and along cliffs as it carries travelers to one of St Croix's most popular attractions, the **Annaly Bay Tide Pools**.

These clear pools in the rocky coastline are teeming with colorful fish, corals and crustaceans. A sprinkling of 4WD vehicles can be found parked along the shell-strewn beach leading to the pools; yet hiking gives you the opportunity to immerse yourself in the rainforest and investigate its smaller creatures – such as reptiles, insects and birds. Novice hikers might consider taking a guide, as rough seas can create dangerous conditions on the rocks.

Alternatively, **Tan Tan Jeep Tours** (stxtantantours.com) runs car-based tours to Annaly Bay. These are especially powerful experiences, as owner Wave Phillips and many of the team at Tan Tan are descendants of people brought to the islands by the transatlantic slave trade, whose voices are not always heard by USVI tourists. Tan Tan's 4WD expeditions traverse lush rainforests, seaside hideaways and former plantations, often ascending to lofty peaks far above the coastline. The team's local insight into the area makes this trip a perfect introduction to St Croix and is an ideal way to start your visit.

🌱 The Caledonia Rainforest

Just south from Annaly Bay, in the island's wet and mountainous northwestern highlands, is the Caledonia Rainforest, a thick woodland of mahogany, silk-cotton and white-cedar trees. Only about 40in of rain falls here per year, so Caledonia is not technically a true rainforest. No matter – it looks the part, with clouds, dripping trees and earthy aromas. Mahogany Rd (Rte 76) cuts through the spooky woods; it's twisty and potholed, so be careful as you drive. A great stop in the forest is **St Croix Leap**, a workshop where local artists create wooden crafts and functional objects out of fallen and upcycled mahogany.

18 Explore Historic
FREDERIKSTED

HISTORY | BEACHES | LGBTQ+

Perhaps because St Croix drifts by its lonesome 40 miles south of the other Virgins, the vibe here is noticeably different: it feels less touristy, less congested, and more 'lived in' by locals. Nowhere is that more apparent than Frederiksted, the quieter West End counterpart to Christiansted, where only the occasional cruise ship gliding in will kick up the pace.

How to

When to go Frederiksted is a late-riser, so best not to start your walk too early. Some business close in low season (July to October).

Getting there Vitran (*dpw.vi.gov*) buses link Christiansted with Frederiksted five times daily. The trip takes about an hour.

Cruises The streets of Frederiksted can feel a bit overrun when a cruise is in town; check the latest schedule with the **VI Port Authority** (*viport.com*).

St Croix's second-banana town is a motionless patch of colonial buildings snoring beside the teal-blue sea. Begin your stroll at the Danish-built **Fort Frederik**. Painted in a deep red hue, it's where the island's enslaved people were emancipated in 1848. Exhibits on the

self-guided tour explain this event, and there is also a small art gallery worth exploring. The fort lies just north of the island's only **cruise pier**, which is also a popular spot for diving.

With its out-of-the-mainstream, laissez-faire ambience, Frederiksted is the

center for gay life in the Virgin Islands and home to many artists. Mosey along Strand and King Sts and you'll find most of the shops, cafes and Caribbean restaurants. Don't miss the **Caribbean Museum Center for the Arts** (*cmcarts.org*), one of the most important cultural

🐴 Cowgirls on Cowboy Beach

The **Cruzan Cowgirls** (*cruzancowgirls.com*) is a Frederiksted organization that rehabilitates malnourished and abused horses across St Croix. A guided trail ride through the rainforest and along the coast at, where else, Cowboy Beach helps fund that work. Horse hooves clip-clop along dirt paths while birds chirp and insects buzz as the natural sounds of St Croix come to life. Riders can feel the salty breeze blowing in across the Caribbean and inhale the scent as it mixes with the sweet fragrance of tropical flowers from wild ginger. The departure point is about 1.5 miles north of town.

institutions in the USVI. Further south, the adults-only beachfront hotels **Sand Castle on the Beach** and **Fred** are the heart of the gay scene, with happening bars and occasional drag shows.

Keep heading south for the total escape that is **Sandy Point National Wildlife Refuge** (*fws.gov/refuge/sandy_point*), a park created to protect nesting areas of the vulnerable leatherback sea turtle, as well as the most pristine stretch of sand on the island. Remember the final scene from *The Shawshank Redemption*? This is where it was shot!

Above Frederiksted

How Virgin are the Islands?

ENVIRONMENTAL WINS, ONGOING CHALLENGES AND A LOOK AHEAD

The 50 or so islands and cays that make up the USVI are the northernmost isles in the Lesser Antilles chain. Each holds a rich array of wildlife both above the sea and below. While a good chunk of the territory is protected as parkland, many environmental threats remain.

Left Buck Island Reef National Monument (p98) **Center** Iguana **Right** Underwater, St Thomas (p42)

CHRIS ALLAN/SHUTTERSTOCK

Protected Lands

The USVI holds a surprising six national park units protecting both historical and natural landmarks. Chief among them are St Croix's Buck Island Reef National Monument and St John's Virgin Islands National Park, which covers two-thirds of that island.

The USVI islands have hilly slopes of dense subtropical forests, most of which is second- or third-growth since all islands in this chain were stripped for sugar, cotton and tobacco plantations in the colonial era. There are no rivers and only a few freshwater streams. Coral reefs of all varieties grow in the shallow waters near the shore.

Wildlife

Very few of the land mammals that make their home in the US Virgin Islands are indigenous; most mammal species were accidentally or intentionally introduced over the centuries. St John has a feral population of donkeys and pigs, and all the islands have wild goats, white-tailed deer, cats and dogs. Other prevalent land mammals include mongooses and bats.

The islands are home to a few species of snake (none of which are venomous), including the Virgin Islands tree boa. You'll also see native frogs, toads, iguanas, anoles, geckos and hermit crabs. More than 200 bird species – including the official bird, the bananaquit – inhabit the islands.

Environmental Issues

The US Virgin Islands have long suffered from environmental problems, including deforestation, soil erosion, mangrove destruction and a lack of fresh water. During the 18th century, logging operations denuded many of the islands to make

room for plantations. The demise of the agricultural economy in the late 19th century allowed reforestation, and locals (especially on St John) have begun several forest-conservation projects.

But population growth and rapid urbanization continue to pose threats. If it were not for the desalination plants (which make fresh water out of seawater), the islands couldn't support even a quarter of their population, let alone visitors. When a hurricane strikes, power and desalination facilities shut down. Some have rainwater cisterns for such emergencies, but folks without them suffer.

> Even the local government has sounded the alarm.

Rising sea temperatures are another topic of concern, as they impact local reefs and cause coral bleaching. In 2005 a particularly hot period killed about half of the USVI's coral. Other widespread bleaching events occurred in 2010, 2019 and 2024. Prior years of overfishing have put conch in a precarious situation. Currently, conch fishing is not allowed from June through October so that stocks can replenish.

A Look Ahead

The past decade has seen an increase in the resources and action dedicated to conservation efforts. Friends of Virgin Islands National Park (*friendsvinp.org*) is a local group that has pushed for better environmental protections, while the Nature Conservancy (*nature.org*) has made the USVI a focal point of its groundbreaking coral-restoration work. Even the local government has sounded the alarm, enacting a ban on plastic shopping bags in 2017 and taking aim at plastic straws in 2018. More recently, lawmakers voted to ban common chemical-sunscreen ingredients that can damage coral reefs.

The Tourism Commissioner's Favorite Experiences

Carnival Celebrations
There's nothing like Carnival in the USVI. Each island has its own, filled with music, moko jumbies (stilt walkers), food, and a deep sense of pride in our traditions.

Trunk Bay, St John
With clear waters, soft sand and a unique snorkeling trail, it's one of the most stunning ways to experience the island's natural beauty.

Frederiksted Pier, St Croix
I love ending the day here with a sunset swim and a taste of local flavors nearby. Nothing feels more like home.

Mountain Top, St Thomas
The view never gets old – and neither does the original banana daiquiri. A classic island moment.

Recommended by **Joseph Boschulte**, USVI Commissioner of Tourism. *dot.vi.govi*

Listings

BEST OF THE REST

 Caribbean Goods

Riddims

Good source for reggae and *quelbe* music from the Virgin Islands, plus clothing, hats, incense and other Caribbean cultural items. The shop also helps sponsor occasional reggae/dub festivals around the island. Ask staff for the lowdown on the local scene.

Many Hands Gallery

Handmade items from local artists and artisans is the name of the game at this small Christiansted shop, which claims that every item has a story behind it.

 More Attractions

Protestant Cay

This small oval cay, located less than 200yd from Kings Wharf in Christiansted, is a little oasis with a sandy beach and hotel bar-restaurant that's open to the public. The ferry (US$5 round trip, five minutes) departs from the wharf.

St George Village Botanical Garden

This serene 16-acre park is built over a colonial sugar plantation. More than 1000 native and exotic species grow on the grounds. Orchid-lovers in particular are in for a treat.

Estate Mount Washington Plantation

Estate Mount Washington lived many lives as a cotton plantation (1750–79), a sugar plantation (1779–1912) and a rum distillery (1780–1860) before it became a citrus farm in 1986. The ruins are on private property, but you're allowed to visit as long as you don't touch the fruit.

Shoy Beach

One of the finest still-wild stretches of sand near Christiansted. There's free parking, plenty of shade, and decent snorkeling at the reefs on either end.

 More Adventures

Paul & Jill's Equestrian Stables

This outfit offers trail rides that lead through hidden plantation ruins and the rainforest to hilltop vistas. You'll also trot along the beach.

Sea-Thru Kayaks VI

Sea-Thru runs tours of bioluminescent Salt River Bay in ubercool clear kayaks so that you can see what's gliding around and beneath you. Call for times and other details.

St Croix Hiking Association

Sponsors a couple of guided hikes per month. They're in offbeat locales, are moderately strenuous, and take three to five hours.

St Croix Environmental Association

Offers two-hour hiking, birdwatching, kayaking and snorkeling trips a few times a month. Many are free; some cost a small fee, depending on the activity.

EA GIVEN/SHUTTERSTOCK ©

Protestant Cay

 Local Cuisine

Singh's Fast Food $

When the roti craving strikes – and it will – Singh's will satiate it with multiple meat and tofu varieties. The steamy three-table joint also serves shrimp, conch, goat and tofu stews, all while island music ricochets off the pastel walls.

Toast Diner $

This teensy, brightly colored spot focuses on (belt-expanding) all-day breakfasts. Hash browns and rum-cake French toast are specialties, as are arepas (South American corn pancakes) with fillings such as pork and *queso fresco* cheese.

Ital in Paradise $$$

This tiny Rasta eatery serves daily platters with both fish and vegan (usually tofu) options. They come with sides such as collard greens, fried lentils and garden salads. Portions are big and delicious. You can eat in at one of the four cramped tables, but many people carry out.

Savant $$$

Cozy, low-lit Savant serves upscale fusion cooking in a colonial town house. The ever-changing menu combines spicy Caribbean, Mexican and Thai recipes; sweat over them indoors in the air-conditioning or outdoors in the courtyard under twinkling lights.

Tropical Cocktails

Rhythms at Rainbow Beach $

Chow down on the signature jerk pork and rice at a table overlooking the sea. Then, let the day turn to night as you toss back tropical

Mt Victory Camp

cocktails and bounce to the beat of blasting reggae at this always-throbbing beach bar 1 mile north of downtown Frederiksted.

Camp or Glamp in a Rainforest

Mt Victory Camp $

Pitch your own tent in the forest, or choose one of three bungalows (screened-in permatents on a wooden platform, each with electricity and a kitchen with cold-water sink, propane stove and cooking utensils). Guests share the solar-heated bathhouse, a pavilion with refrigerator and wi-fi, and sublime nature sounds.

Ridge to Reef Farm $

Tour an organic farm in St Croix's rainforest, either on your own (with a map) or with a guide (reservations required). You can also work in the fields or stay overnight; lodging is provided in one of six rustic though totally adequate cabins, or in your own tent.

LEON WERDINGER/ALAMY

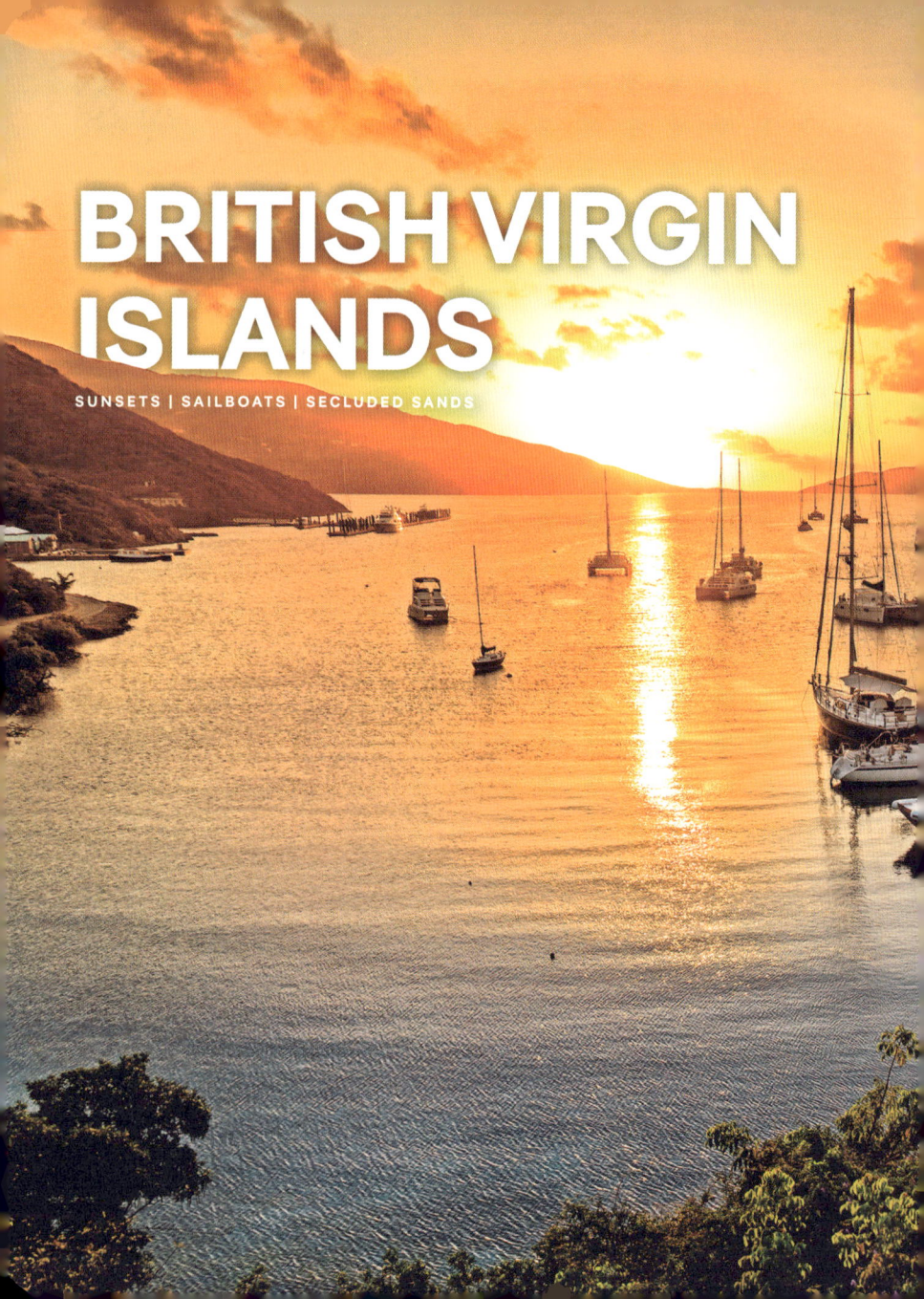

BRITISH VIRGIN ISLANDS

SUNSETS | SAILBOATS | SECLUDED SANDS

▸ **Tortola** (p118)

▸ **Virgin Gorda** (p146)

▸ **Anegada** (p164)

▸ **Jost Van Dyke** (p182)

Practicalities

SERGEY KELIN/SHUTTERSTOCK

ARRIVING

Air Regular flights from the US and Europe arrive at **Terrance B Lettsome International Airport**. Fly in and hop on a ferry or charter to Virgin Gorda, or take a taxi via the bridge that connects Tortola to Beef Island.

Boat Road Town hosts the BVI's most-used cruise port (pictured). There's a modern outdoor mall of global brands dockside, though the town is within walking distance. Moorings for private vessels abound, giving those with a sailing spirit nearly limitless places to land.

HOW MUCH FOR A...

painkiller US$9

plate of conch fritters US$15

dinghy rental US$100

GETTING AROUND

Taxi Uber won't work here. The best alternative to ride-share is to grab the WhatsApp number of a respected taxi driver. This will burn through dollar bills, but can pay off with local knowledge and insights.

Boat Daily ferries run from Tortola to Jost Van Dyke and Virgin Gorda. Every few days, a ferry heads off for Anegada, too. Private charters can get you from place to place on your own time for a premium fee.

Rental Renting a car makes a lot of sense on both Tortola and Virgin Gorda. On Anegada, swap the car for a scooter or moke. Rates offer good value when compared to cab fares.

WHEN TO GO

DEC–FEB
Peak season means top-notch weather and top-notch prices.

MAR–JUN
Temperatures and humidity rise, but prices dip somewhat.

JUL–SEP
Hotter, stickier conditions make for fewer crowds and good deals. Some outfitters will be closed.

OCT–NOV
Off-season means rain. Many hotels or charters will be closed for renovations or refitting.

EATING & DRINKING

The cuisine of the British Virgin Islands reflects a rich blend of African, Caribbean and European influences. Seafood plays a central role, with dishes like grilled lobster, conch stew and fish soup being staples. Local ingredients such as plantains, yams and callaloo (a leafy green) feature heavily, often served with rice and peas. Food is both a communal and celebratory experience, with beach barbecues, fish fries and food festivals being common.

Best surprise steak and peaches
Mountain View Restaurant (p133)

Must-try painkiller cocktail
Soggy Dollar Bar (p187; pictured)

CONNECT & FIND YOUR WAY

Wi-fi 5G and LTE services are generally spotty in the BVI. Expect to find coverage along beaches and near major towns, but you'll lose it in the mountains and offshore.

Navigation Smartphone navigation apps work in the BVI. Get directions before you leave service areas. Consider downloading AllTrails for hiking or Navionics for paddle sports.

SAFETY

Exercise normal precautions in the BVI. Crime levels are generally low, but bag snatching and pickpocketing can occur. If chartering a yacht, pay special attention to the booking agency's safety record.

WHERE TO STAY

Accommodations in the BVI range from two-star hotels that get the job done to ultra-luxury, five-star resorts with helipads. There's an option here for almost everyone.

Town/Area	Pros/Cons
Carrot Bay	Upscale villas wedged between jungle peaks and Tortola's famous surf breaks.
Soper's Hole	Private vacation rentals with easy access to ferries and marinas on Tortola's West End.
White Bay	Quiet getaway on Jost Van Dyke, right between the most famous bars in the BVI.
Spanish Town	Budget-friendly, locally run hotels within a short drive of Virgin Gorda's natural wonders.
Private yacht	Anchor anywhere you find a mooring and spend the night beside uninhabited islands.

MONEY

Credit cards are widely accepted, but cash comes in handy – especially at beach bars. ATMs can be found in major settlements, but may or may not be in working order; make a withdrawal when you see an opportunity.

TORTOLA

SURF SPOTS | MANGROVES | CITY STREETS

RESEARCHED BY JOE SILLS

▶ **Trip Builder** (p120)

▶ **Practicalities** (p121)

▶ **Wander the Waterfront in Road Town** (p122)

▶ **Revel at the Regatta** (p124)

▶ **Learn to Surf in Josiah's Bay** (p126)

▶ **Explore Secluded Bays & Coves** (p128)

▶ **Rewriting Maritime History** (p130)

▶ **The Lost World of Sage Mountain** (p132)

▶ **Find Paradise on the North Shore** (p134)

▶ **Paddleboard a Shark Nursery** (p136)

▶ *Gli Gli*: **A Journey Through Time, Sea & Memory** (p138)

▶ **Listings** (p140)

Atlantic
Ocean

Spend a day
at the beach
at **Apple Bay**
(p135).
🚗 *20 min
from Road Town*

Learn to surf
or hit the point
break at **Josiah's
Bay** (p126).
🚗 *20 min from
Road Town*

*Guana
Island*

*Great
Camanoe*

*Little
Camanoe*

*Scrub
Island*

*Beef
Island*

° East End

🏄

🍴🍹⚓ **Road Town**

Walk the
waterfront of
Road Town
(p122; pictured
below) and grab
a painkiller at
Pusser's.

🚶 *Sage
Mountain*

B R I T I S H   V I R G I N
I S L A N D S   (U K)

*Caribbean
Sea*

*Great
Thatch*

*Little
Thatch*

☀️

° West End

*Frenchmans
Cay*

Hike along the jungle trails
of **Sage Mountain** (p132)
and cool off with a fresh
banana smoothie.
🚗 *25 min from Road Town*

*Peter
Island*

Catch the sunset beside
the sparkling white sands
of **Smuggler's Cove** (p129;
pictured above).
🚗 *45 min from Road Town*

U S   V I R G I N
I S L A N D S
(U S)

TORTOLA
Trip Builder

▬▬▬ Tortola, the most populous BVI, offers winding
roads, vibrant Road Town nightlife, secluded North
Shore getaways, surf spots, and ferries to other major
islands. This mountainous Caribbean paradise blends
adventure, quiet escapes and diverse cuisines with
vibrant, rugged peaks and a busy cruise port.

5 km
2.5 miles

Practicalities

ARRIVING

Terrance B Lettsome International Airport The only international airport in the BVI offers the country's fastest entry.

Road Town Ferry Terminal Ferries from the USVI arrive here or at **West End Ferry Terminal** near Soper's Hole.

FIND YOUR WAY

Google and Apple Maps do work on Tortola. Expect winding roads of varying condition and quality, and erratic driving habits.

MONEY

Save money by packing lunches, avoiding long cab rides, or pooling together with friends to book an all-inclusive charter yacht.

WHERE TO STAY

Area	Pros/Cons
Soper's Hole	Charming Frenchman's Cay community with vacation rentals, coffee shops and its own Pusser's.
Cane Garden	Stellar beaches and luxury hotels with a pint-sized beach nightlife scene.
Road Town	More cost-friendly hotels that serve as base camps for adventures elsewhere.

EATING & DRINKING

Must-visit spots include the **Sugar Mill**, famed for lobster bisque and rum-glazed pork. At **Quito's Gazebo**, savor grilled mahi-mahi with Creole sauce, while **D'Coalpot** serves authentic goat curry and fungi (cornmeal mash). For beachside dining, try **Omar's Fusion** (pictured top) for fresh snapper and plantains. And visit **Crandall's Pastry Plus** in Road Town for the best johnnycakes.

Best painkiller
Pusser's (p123; pictured)

Must-try roti
Naturally Tasti (p140)

GETTING AROUND

Ferry Speedy's, Native Son and Road Town Fast Ferry are the dominant means of island-hopping in the BVI. Plan to pay a premium.

Rental car Maximum flexibility, and rates are usually cheaper than if you were to take a handful of cab rides per day.

Taxi The most convenient way to get around is also the most expensive.

TORTOLA FIND YOUR FEET

NOV–APR
Lobster Festival and the BVI Spring Sailing Regatta bookend peak season.

MAY–JUL
Summer means calm seas, full-moon parties and BVI Wreck Week.

AUG–OCT
Hurricane season brings prime fishing runs but dicey conditions for beachgoers.

Wander the Waterfront in
ROAD TOWN

SHOPPING | DINING | NIGHTLIFE

In Road Town, you'll find the bars, restaurants, banks and stores that fuel life on Tortola. While the city of about 15,000 is more known for commercial activity than charm, Road Town is an essential pit stop while visiting the island. Swing by Tortola Cruise Ship Pier for souvenirs like magnets and stickers, or grab a seaside rum punch at Pusser's restaurant.

🗺 How to

Getting here & around
It's easy to explore Road Town on foot or grab a cab near the docks. Cruise passengers arrive on Tortola directly from the city's cruise ship port. International chains like Enterprise and Avis all provide rental car services.

When to go First thing off the ferry.

Busy streets Road Town can feel like the only crowded place in the BVI, and open-air taxis abound near the cruise port.

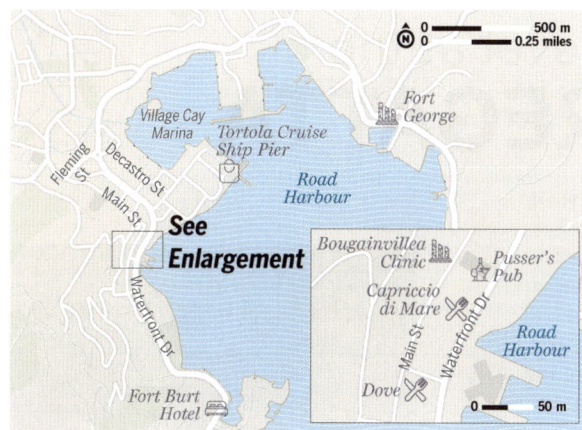

Far left top Tortola Cruise Ship Pier
Far left bottom Road Town shopping

Tortola's Chaotic Heart

Road Town is the honking, churning, chaotic heart of Tortola. While most of the island is renowned for relaxation, this port is a place where business gets done. It's a place to rent a car, connect with a cab driver or make a withdrawal from the bank; but that doesn't mean Road Town is completely without charm.

At times, its harbor glows gold, sailboats swaying gently in a breeze scented with salt and hibiscus. Along Main Street, pastel buildings lean lazily under the weight of time, their shutters thrown open to welcome the day. Curbside ice-cream vendors ready their wares and souvenir shops begin to open their doors.

Waterfront Restaurants

If you're arriving on a ferry, try wandering across the street over to the **Dove**. This island staple sits in a clapboard building less than a minute from the ferry terminal. Try the tuna tartare – fresh, bright, kissed with sesame and lime – and set the tone for an unhurried afternoon. A two-minute walk away, **Pusser's Pub** anchors the waterfront with legendary painkillers – a potent blend of rum, coconut and spice with the power to put even the most staunch micromanager on island time.

At night, the streets of Road Town swell with sound. Steel drums echo through shaded alleys while the smell of wood-fired pizza rises from **Capriccio di Mare**, where patrons linger over grilled grouper and limoncello spritz.

Ruins of Road Town

Remnants of Road Town's sordid past are obscured by the bustle of modern commerce. However, the overgrown remains of **Fort George**, believed to have been built in part by Dutch settlers in the 17th century, are still visible.

The last significant fort built in Road Town now serves as part of the foundation for the **Bougainvillea Clinic**, a private hospital. Some of the original fort walls are visible from Main St.

You can stay in the **Fort Burt Hotel** (fortburt.com), on top of the ruins of a colonial-era British fort that was built at the onset of the American War of Independence in 1776.

20

Revel at the
REGATTA

MUSIC | SAILING | CELEBRATION

For one week each year, a secluded Tortola cay becomes an epicenter of sailing, singing and celebration. Make your way to the southern shore of the island in the waning days of spring to join the fray at Nanny Cay. Here, a backdrop of jungle-encrusted mountain peaks forms a mosaic celebration to sailing over sapphire waters and the rum runners.

How to

Getting here Sailors can moor at Nanny Cay. Land-lovers can take a 20-minute cab from Road Town (US$30) or rent their own vehicle near the Road Town Cruise Pier.

When to go The BVI Spring Regatta usually takes place at the end of March or beginning of April. Check bvispringregatta.org for precise dates.

Accommodations Book lodging in advance for one of the biggest parties in the BVI.

JORNO/SHUTTERSTOCK

In late spring, the breeze off Nanny Cay fills the sails of dozens of yachts, big and small. The BVI Spring Regatta is one of the world's great festivals of sailing.

Fueled by the BVI's legendary sailing conditions, this week of fun revolves around Nanny Cay, where sailors from every corner of the globe descend to race around Tortola. Masts sway like metronomes, rigging clinks in rhythm, and spinnakers bloom bright against the sky. An on-site Regatta Village with concerts, drinks and vendors pops up by the docks, giving landlubbers and seafarers a place to mingle.

Fun for Salty Dogs & Land-Lovers

For seven days, Sir Francis Drake Channel fills with sleek hulls cutting through turquoise swells, chasing wind around designated courses. Spectators gather along the docks, on charter boats or in the beachside bars, eyes tracing the dance

FRANK LERVIK/SHUTTERSTOCK

⛵ A Sailor's Paradise

The **BVI Spring Regatta** began in 1972 as a modest sailing event, drawing a handful of local yachts to the turquoise waters of Tortola. Over the decades, it has grown into one of the Caribbean's premier sailing festivals, attracting top-tier racers and cruising enthusiasts from around the world.

The BVI are world-renowned for sailing, thanks to consistent trade winds, calm seas and the close proximity of more than 60 picturesque islands. Yachts are a common sight here, drawn in by the sheltered anchorages, crystal-clear waters, and scenic routes through the Sir Francis Drake Channel that make the BVI a sailor's paradise.

of sails against the horizon. Sailors can join in on the fun by renting a yacht in Nanny Cay from Bareboat Charters, BVI Yacht Charters or Island Time BVI.

When the sun dips low and anchors drop, Nanny Cay comes alive with a different kind of magic. The Regatta Village pulses with music, laughter and the easy clink of glasses raised high. At **Peg Legs Restaurant**, stories are traded over plates of conch fritters and fresh lobster, while the rum flows freely, warming the salt-stung skin of sailors and spectators alike.

Left Yachts, Tortola
Above Nanny Cay marina

21

Learn to Surf in
JOSIAH'S BAY

SURF WAX | SWELLS | VIBES

A skateboard ramp and crashing waves greet visitors to Josiah's Bay, where Surf School BVI has set up shop in a pair of shipping containers. Inside, you'll find friendly staff, a selection of drinks and a library of travel books. Surf School BVI has a prime position along Tortola's northern coastline, where swells crash year-round. Bring your swimsuit and your best vibes.

POELIZER WOLFGANG/ALAMY

📷 How to

Getting here The best way to get here is by driving or hiring a cab. If you choose a cab, save the driver's contact info for the return trip.

When to go Call the surf school in advance to see if conditions are prime.

Top tip Surf lessons start at US$60 for up to two hours, but students are free to linger around the school (and firepit) all day.

ARTERRA PICTURE LIBRARY/ALAMY

JOE SILLS/LONELY PLANET

Far left top and bottom Josiah's Bay
Left Surf School BVI

Sun's Up, Surf's Up

About 20 minutes by car from the clubs of Road Town, Josiah's Bay hums with an island rhythm of its own – waves crash, boards carve, and laughter echoes from a weathered skate ramp. Here, **Surf School BVI** (*surfschoolbvi.vg*) rises from a pair of shipping containers like a phoenix of saltwater and stoke. South African expat Steve Howes, Jamaican surf legend Icah Wilmot and local wave-rider Alex Dick-Read hold court just steps from the sea, guiding surfers across a reef break that churns year-round.

Back in 2017 hurricanes Irma and Maria tried to wipe this place off the map. But the trio stayed, rebuilding their dream wave by wave. Now, a lifeguard chair perches atop a new viewing deck, watching over sets that peel under Caribbean skies.

All Skill Levels Welcome

Whether you're a greenhorn or a seasoned shredder, there's a break with your name on it. Beginners ease into a gentle roll near the beach, while veterans chase bigger lines off a nearby point break. Between sessions, surfers flip through tattered surf mags and travel guides, swap tales around a driftwood fire, or chill with a cold drink from the beach bar.

And when the sea rests, the bay offers another peace – lines cast into quiet waters, the hum of the island in your bones. Booking? Easy. Drop by, email or hit up Howes on WhatsApp. The waves are waiting.

✎ Surviving then Thriving

In 2017 Josiah's Bay was rocked by Hurricane Irma, the first recorded Category 5 hurricane to ever hit the Leeward Islands.

Inside a small cove on the northern shore of Tortola, a fledgling surf school built along the shore was wiped off the map. During the storm, the shipping container that houses much of the surf school was washed inland, wrecking most of the gear inside. But Tortola wouldn't let the surf school die. Volunteers came unbidden to help rebuild the school and replenish its inventory for events like the now annual **Josiah's Bay Surf Classic**, held each spring.

22 Explore Secluded
BAYS & COVES

SNORKELING | BEACH CHAIRS | PAINKILLERS

Spend a day chasing sun and salt on Tortola's wilder north shore. The secluded sands of Smuggler's Cove and the reef-filled waters of Brewers Bay offer a laid-back escape from the grind. Expect dusty roads, strong rum drinks and natural beauty. Out here, the vibe is chill, and the best plan is no plan.

DENNIS MACDONALD/SHUTTERSTOCK

📷 **How to**

Getting here Taxi services can ferry you to these further-afield locations, but expect to pay at least US$100 for the round trip. Rental cars are the best option – just be sure to designate a driver.

When to go Year-round, though you may want to plan to arrive well before sunset. Remote bars sometimes close at dusk.

On the menu Beach bar menus vary by whims and daily catches. Be flexible.

MAURITIUS IMAGES GMBH/ALAMY

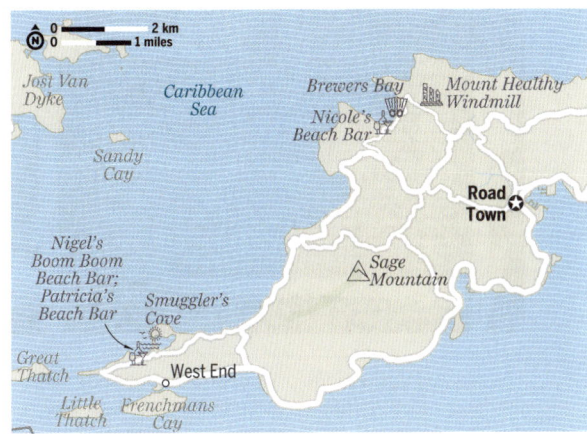

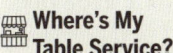

Far left top Smuggler's Cove
Far left bottom Brewers Bay

Tortola's north shore is well known for consistent northern swells, but several secluded bays offer tranquil beaches with lapping shorelines just minutes from the surf breaks at Josiah's Bay, Apple Bay and Cane Garden.

Enter **Smuggler's Cove**. The road there isn't pretty: it's a rugged, bone-rattling trail over rocky creek crossings and leaning palms, the kind of drive that makes you wonder if you took a wrong turn. But trust it – at the end, the chaos opens up to one of Tortola's best beaches. Smuggler's Cove is a slice of unfiltered Caribbean. No crowds, no cruise ship vibes – just soft white sand, calm turquoise water and the sway of sea grape bushes.

Nigel's Boom Boom Beach Bar will set you up with beach chairs and an ice-cold painkiller, heavy on the nutmeg. Nigel might even grill you some fish or ribs if you ask nicely. It's that kind of place.

When you're sun-soaked and salty, point your rental car east to **Brewers Bay**, about 20 minutes east beneath the ruins of the 18th-century **Mount Healthy Windmill**. Protected by shallow, barrier reefs, the beach here offers some of the best snorkeling on Tortola. Bring your own gear and paddle out. The reef covers most of the bay, and it's alive with coral, reef fish and the occasional sea turtle. When you're ready to dry off, **Nicole's Beach Bar** can set you up with snacks and drinks.

These beaches aren't polished, but that's the point. Bring cash. Bring a cooler. Leave the resort mindset behind.

🏚 Where's My Table Service?

Throughout the Caribbean, roadside shacks and surfside beach bars built of plywood, corrugated metal and concrete blocks pepper the landscape. Typically, they serve up limited menus of conch salad or whatever fish can be thrown on the grill.

While not as polished as swim-up bars at all-inclusive resorts, these bars are a part of the true Caribbean experience. As a general rule of thumb: the more homemade the bar appears, the better the drinks tend to be. An afternoon spent with sandy toes at spots like **Nicole's**, **Nigel's** or **Patricia's Beach Bar** delivers a true taste of the Caribbean spirit.

Rewriting Maritime History

HISTORIC RECORDS SHOWCASE INDIGENOUS INGENUITY ON THE ISLANDS

Often, the maritime history of the Caribbean seems to start with an Italian explorer from Genoa arriving on these shores under Spanish sails. But Columbus was far from the first mariner to ply these waters. Modern research and archaeological evidence reveals that the Indigenous people of the Virgin Islands were experts at seafaring.

Left Columbus landing site, Salt River Bay National Historic Park (p105) **Center** Depiction of Columbus and Taíno people by artist Sasso **Right** Petroglyph

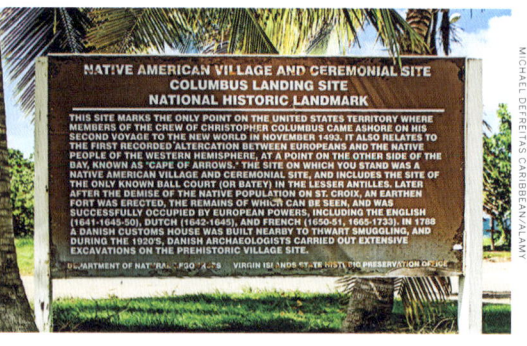

The sea was their roadmap. Before Columbus and colonial flags laid claim to their homelands, the Indigenous peoples of the Caribbean carved a life from the ocean here. Estimates put the population of Indigenous people living in the Caribbean as high as one million souls before Columbus arrived. And those souls had stories.

Their stories were not written in books but carried on the waves, passed from canoe to canoe, island to island. The British Virgin Islands, now a haven for sailors and sun-seekers, once formed a vital node in an ancient network of seafaring cultures.

For centuries, the narrative of Caribbean history centered on Columbus. But long before 1493, when Columbus first sighted the Virgin Islands, these waters were alive with movement. The Arawak-speaking Taíno, and later the Kalinago (Caribs), navigated hundreds of miles of open sea in dugout canoes carved from silk cotton trees.

A Trail of Archaeological Clues

Archaeological findings and re-examinations of oral traditions are beginning to shift our understanding of these early mariners. The people who lived in the Virgin Islands weren't isolated. They were part of a sophisticated web of trade stretching from the Greater Antilles to the northern coast of South America. They moved with the currents, trading pottery, cotton, cassava and stories, building a culture that was as fluid as the sea they called home.

In the Virgin Islands, evidence of this history lingers just beneath the modern surface. The archaeological record suggests the presence of temporary fishing camps in the archipelago as early as 1500 BCE. And it's believed that

Arawak people first arrived to settle on the islands around 200 BCE, some 1500 years before Columbus arrived.

Yet, the dominant historical narrative has downplayed the seafaring skills of these Indigenous cultures, portraying them as passive inhabitants of paradise, caught unawares by European expansion.

This view is changing. Recent research has revealed that these were master navigators, capable of reading the winds and stars with a precision that modern sailors still strive to understand. Their canoes, described by early Europeans as swift and graceful, were not simple rafts but carefully crafted tools of exploration and connection.

> Recent research has revealed that these were master navigators

Honoring Ancestry Through Craft

Today, the descendants of those first Caribbean sailors are reclaiming their place in history. Across the region, efforts are underway to revive traditional canoe building – like the shipyard at Aragorn's Studio (p138) on Beef Island – to teach new generations the skills of their ancestors.

The polished, glossy veneer of the British Virgin Islands can be deceiving. These islands are more than a playground for yachts and regattas. They are part of a larger, older story – a story of human ingenuity, of cultures built on the water, of people who understood that the sea could carry you home if you knew how to listen. As the winds fill the sails of modern boats racing across the Sir Francis Drake Channel, they follow in the wake of those ancient mariners, whose feats are only now being more widely appreciated.

Columbus in the Virgin Islands

Columbus brought more than a name to the BVI. He also brought conflict. On his second voyage to the Americas, Columbus dropped anchor off St Croix with 17 ships, claiming the island for Spain. While carrying residents of a nearby village back to his fleet, Columbus exchanged gunpowder and arrow volleys with a canoe of Carib residents, killing two people.

Visit the site, called the Cape of Arrows, at Salt River Bay National Historical Park and Ecological Reserve. Hop a ferry to St Thomas and on to St Croix from Road Town or the West End.

23

The Lost World of
SAGE MOUNTAIN

JUNGLES | SMOOTHIES | PIÑA COLADAS

A surreal hike through Tortola's dense, moody banana forest may lure you to the top of Sage Mountain. A mercurial chef manning a solitary restaurant on its summit will keep you lingering there through the night.

JASON PATRICK ROSS/SHUTTERSTOCK

📍 **How to**

Getting here Cabs from Road Town can ferry you to Sage Mountain in about 25 minutes (US$10). You can also flag a passing bus and tell the driver you want to go to Sage Mountain.

When to go Early afternoon, to bask in the shade of the banana leaves.

Top tip Visit Mountain View Restaurant and talk to Jim. He'll offer you a chance to book a dinner reservation.

JASON PATRICK ROSS/SHUTTERSTOCK

Far left top View of Tortola from Sage Mountain National Park **Far left bottom and left** Sage Mountain National Park

The Guardian of the Forest

A left turn at the rooster hanging by the dumpster on Ridge Rd will send you to the gates of **Sage Mountain National Park**. Jim Cullimore will be waiting for you there, holding a hand-drawn map and a blender. Jim runs **Mountain View Restaurant**, and the retired Royal Navy chef has become something of a guardian for the surrounding park and its visitors.

Swing a left inside the restaurant's open front door and you'll bump right into the bar. This is Jim's domain. From this room, stories of his banana smoothies have spread to become legendary lore for cruise passengers on safari tours of Tortola. The refreshingly cool bite of the smoothies come with commanding views of Sir Francis Drake Passage and the crashing Caribbean Sea some 1700ft below.

X Marks the Dining Room

The misty, muddy paths of Sage Mountain National Park hold an abundance of secrets, illuminated by the rays piercing its lush canopy of banana leaves. Jim knows this. And he knows that the trails here are not particularly well marked. To solve this riddle, Jim dispenses free maps of the meandering trail system inside of the adjacent park. His hand-drawn directions may be the best way to navigate to sights like the highest point in the British Virgin Islands and the majestic, ancient gum tree dominating a slice of path deep inside the canopy.

Return the pages of the maps intact, and Jim might just invite you in for a home-cooked dinner if he takes an interest in your journey.

Flora & Fauna of Sage Mountain

Imagine stepping into a lush, green paradise, where towering mahogany trees, ancient West Indian gum trees and giant elephant ear ferns create a canopy so dense it's like a natural ceiling. Wild orchids hide in the shadows, while vines drape like curtains across muddy trails. The air is filled with the chirping of birds – keep your eyes peeled for the green-throated carib, Caribbean doves, and the elusive Antillean crested hummingbird. Hermit crabs scuttle along the forest floor, and mongoose dart through the bushes. The captivating lost world of Sage Mountain National Park holds enough secrets to lure you away from Tortola's stunning beaches.

24 Find Paradise on the
NORTH SHORE

SEASHELLS | SANDY STROLLS | MUSEUMS

Spend a day exploring Tortola's vibrant west side, where surf meets intriguing museums and local cuisine. From the rolling waves of Apple Bay to the peaceful charm of Carrot Bay, and the golden-hour magic of Cane Garden, it's time well spent.

BCAMPBELL65/SHUTTERSTOCK

📍 How to

Getting here Taxi drivers are more than happy to lighten your purse or wallet to get around the island, but a rental car is the best way to save money and make your own schedule.

When to go Start in the early morning and spend all day by the sea.

Top tip Carry cash. Card readers are more frequently found these days, but cash comes in handy for impromptu tours and beach chairs.

LAZYLLAMA/SHUTTERSTOCK

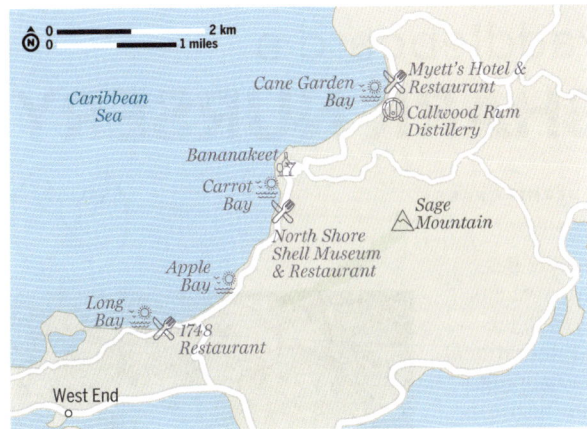

Far left top Carrot Bay
Far left bottom Apple Bay

A day in the North Shore bays is Tortola in three beats: surf, soul and sunsets.

Start your morning with the surf at **Apple Bay**. This spot's for early risers and wave chasers – home to Tortola's most consistent breaks. Even if you're not paddling out, the scene's worth catching. Grab breakfast and a seaside coffee at **1748 Restaurant** at adjacent **Long Bay**, watch the surfers carve the swells, and let the sea breeze wake you up.

Roll west to **Carrot Bay**, a quiet fishing village with a slower feel, for a pit stop at the **North Shore Shell Museum & Restaurant**. Browse the aisles of this roadside shack, where thousands of carefully arranged seashells form a backdrop for local fare like conch curry and soursop juice – a drink made from the indigenous soursop plant (rich in vitamins) that hints of pineapple, strawberry and lime.

By afternoon, make your way over the hill to **Cane Garden Bay**. Widely regarded as Tortola's most scenic beach, Cane Garden is home to a host of beach restaurants and watersports rentals. As you may imagine, the rum flows freely here. Hit up **Myett's Hotel & Restaurant** or walk south along the beach for a 15-minute tour through the ruin-like **Callwood Rum Distillery** (US$5) before a sunset stroll beside the sand. Or walk around the bend to **Bananakeet** for a cold drink while live tunes drift out to sea. .

What's in the Name?

Cane Garden is synonymous with one of the Caribbean's most beautiful beach getaways today. But its name harkens back to a more sinister past. At the beach's southern terminus, a clue to the past sits seemingly crumbling back into the soil – the Callwood Rum Distillery.

Don't come here expecting a grand tour; spend a few bucks for a taste of local rum and a swig of Cane Garden's history. At one time, 106 distilleries operated in the BVI, 26 of them on Tortola. Today, this Cane Garden relic named for a real-life buccaneer is the only one left (sort of) standing.

25

Paddleboard a
SHARK NURSERY

JELLYFISH | SHARK PUPS | HERMIT CRABS

 A nursery for marine life lies hidden behind fleets of luxury yachts and the resting wings of private jets near Terrance B Lettsome International Airport. In coves of shallow, lapping water, a critical frontline for hurricane defense and a nursery for fledgling sea creatures welcomes the occasional group of paddleboarders. Grab a board and see the ocean in a new light.

🗺 How to

Getting here There's no public paddleboard-rental station in Tortola's mangrove forest. To gain access, you'll need to connect with Surf School BVI instructor and **GroundSea Adventures BVI** owner Alex Dick-Read, a former journalist turned eco-tour guide (*groundseabvi.com; US$90*).

When to go Midmorning or midafternoon offers good light for viewing marine life below your board.

Exclusive access GroundSea Adventures has exclusivity at the site. You'll have to book with them.

NATTAPON PONBUMRUNGWONG/SHUTTERSTOCK

What SUP in a Mangroves Forest?

Alex Dick-Read has a love affair with Beef Island, but not for its lofty social status. Alex, who co-operates BVI Surf School, spends much of his time gliding beneath the silhouette of the airport's control tower in the mangrove forest of **Beef Island Lagoon** on a paddleboard.

Thanks to a philanthropic investor, the mangroves here are protected from most developers, offering the area a natural barrier to hurricanes and the effects of climate change a chance to catch up.

The Beef Island mangroves are a nursery for the BVI's marine life. They provide a sanctuary for juvenile lemon sharks, a home for sensitive single-cell organisms, and a haven for crustaceans, jelly-fish and mangrove shoots. Alex says the mangroves here saved the airport from major destruction during back-to-back hurricanes Irma and Maria. The former surf

ODETA LUKOSEVICIUTE/SHUTTERSTOCK

〰 Science in the Lagoon

'In 2022 we started tagging sharks in that area. We were able to definitively prove that it is a lemon shark nursery – one of just three in the BVI. We put tags on sharks that work all around the Americas. So, if one of our sharks shows up in Miami, we know. Years ago, you could probably find the species there in abundance elsewhere in Hans Creek and on Anegada. But it's unique now because we have landfilled everywhere.'

Beyond the Reef co-founder **Chris Juredin** is a citizen scientist studying marine life in the BVI. His group conducts ongoing research in the mangroves. *1BeyondtheReef.com*

magazine editor works with scientists to help restore the delicate ecosystem between bouts with Mother Nature.

How to Get Involved

You can learn more about citizen science in the mangroves by paddling with Dick-Read. On regular, two- to three-hour tours, Dick-Read breaks down the science behind the conservation work while showcasing dozens of species of unique sea creatures using the mangroves as a home.

A short drive from the lagoon, travelers can belly up at the **Loose Mongoose** for famous daiquiris, wood-fired pizza, local beer and lobster.

Left Mangroves **Above** Sharks

Gli Gli: A Journey Through Time, Sea & Memory

WHEN ISLANDERS PROVED THEIR ANCESTORS' SEA SKILLS

The Caribbean's waves once carried canoes, not cruise ships. *Gli Gli*, a modern homage to ancient voyages, braved hundreds of nautical miles to honor the region's first mariners. Her story is one of resilience, tradition, and the sea's role in retying connections lost to colonialism.

RE METALI/SHUTTERSTOCK

The Caribbean doesn't forget. Beneath its turquoise surface and postcard-perfect skies, the sea holds ancient stories. In 1997 one of those stories came roaring back to life, carved from the heart of Dominica's forests and set loose on the ocean that once bound a people together before it tore them apart. That hero of that story was *Gli Gli*, a 35ft-long dugout canoe, born of *gommier* trees and a vision to restore pride in the Caribbean's Indigenous seafaring skills.

Crafted by Jonathan Fredericks of Dominica, *Gli Gli* was a vessel for reclamation. Named after the Carib word for the sparrowhawk, a bird known for its swiftness and sharp gaze, *Gli Gli* was built entirely by hand. Two massive *gommier* trees gave their bodies to its hull. They were hollowed, joined and made strong enough to brave a journey that few would dare in modern times.

With a Caribbean-based crew, including Tortola-born artist Aragorn Dick-Read (Alex's brother), Fredericks set sail from the shores of Dominica, eyes fixed on Venezuela. This wasn't a reenactment for tourists or a ceremonial float – it was a real voyage, through real risks, to reconnect distant Kalinago (Carib) peoples separated by colonial conquest.

The route was ancient. From Dominica, through the Grenadines, past Trinidad, and onward to the mainland coast of South America: the pathway was trod by countless seafarers long before European sails darkened the horizon.

They battled rough seas and trusted the bones of their canoe to carry them approximately 500 nautical miles to the Orinoco Delta, making stops to talk to Indigenous communities about their seafaring past. From the Caribbean,

Left and right *Gli Gli* replica canoes

PRISMA BY DUKAS PRESSEAGENTUR GMBH/ALAMY

Gli Gli traveled through river systems in northwest Guyana to make contact with Kalinago communities in South America.

Their remarkable journey echoed another – Norwegian explorer Thor Heyerdahl's daring expeditions across the Pacific and the Atlantic in primitive vessels. Like *Gli Gli*, Heyerdahl's *Kon-Tiki* raft and later *Ra II* were built using ancient techniques challenging mainstream historical thought. They made bold assertions that early humans from Polynesia and Africa could traverse immense waters long before modern navigation.

> It was united by water, by trade, by shared language and blood.

Gli Gli, in the same breath, stood as a living testament to the endurance of the Indigenous identity of the Caribbean, a reminder that before the region was carved up by empires, it was united by water, by trade, by shared language and blood.

The journey marked a revelation of Caribbean seafaring heritage, not to prove to the world what was possible, but to remind a people of what had always been.

Today, visitors to Beef Island can stop by Aragorn's Studio, a pottery studio that hosts full-moon festivals in a sculpture garden on the shores of Trellis Bay. There, *Gli Gli* rests, her hull weathered but proud after sailing from Dominica to the BVI.

Locals say she is not done yet. Rumors swirl about a new voyage to Cuba and a return to the open sea, where the horizon still calls.

In a world where speed and silicone define progress, *Gli Gli* asks us to look back before we look ahead, to feel the pull of tides that carried Indigenous people across these waters not as obstacles, but as connections.

Gli Gli's Place in History

Gli Gli ranks among the most significant modern sea voyages of traditionally built craft.

Kon-Tiki (1947) 4300 miles from Peru to Polynesia on a balsa wood raft.

Ra II (1970) 3270 miles from Morocco to Barbados on a papyrus boat.

Hōkūle'a (1976) Over 2500 miles across the Pacific from Hawaii to Tahiti.

Makali'i (1995) Multiple voyages, including Hawaii to Tahiti, in a double-hulled canoe.

Gli Gli (1997) 500 miles from Dominica to Venezuela in a Carib dugout canoe.

Olo'upena (2002) Pacific crossings with Micronesian *proas*, distances ranging from 500 to 1500 miles between islands.

Listings

BEST OF THE REST

 Just Off Shore

Guana Island

A private, pristine retreat known for its lush forests, white-sand beaches and nature trails. Guana Island Resort offers eco-luxury lodging. White Bay Beach is the island's main beach, ideal for swimming, snorkeling and relaxing.

Great Camanoe

A residential island popular with sailors and nature-lovers. Accessible only by boat, it features Indigo Plantation, a small private development. Lee Bay is a favorite for anchorage and snorkeling amid vibrant underwater life.

Little Camanoe

Spy this uninhabited, rugged island from Tortola's West End. Its rocky coastline offers limited access but adventurous snorkeling opportunities. Explore quiet, lesser-known coves occasionally used by kayakers and those seeking undisturbed natural beauty.

Scrub Island

Scrub Island features the luxurious Scrub Island Resort, Spa & Marina. This popular overnight destination is famed for turquoise waters and sunbathing, while nearby reefs offer great snorkeling opportunities.

Great Thatch Island

An uninhabited island with dense vegetation and the ruins of a historical customs house. While there are no resorts, the beach on the southern side near the anchorage is popular for snorkeling and day visits by boaters.

Little Thatch

Little Thatch is a small, privately owned island just south of Great Thatch Island. The surrounding reefs make for excellent snorkeling spots.

 Reservations Recommended

Indigo Beach House $

Tucked along Cane Garden Bay, Indigo is a barefoot beachside escape with a rustic charm. It's part supper club, part tropical hideaway. Enjoy fresh conch fritters, cold drinks and ocean breezes just steps from the surf. Sunset is magic.

Naturally Tasti $$

Owned by the charismatic RotiMan, Naturally Tasti is a casual, colorful haven offering roti packed with bold island flavors. Relax under fluttering umbrellas as reggae plays and the breeze rolls in. A quirky, soulful food stop that locals adore.

Marché at Trellis Bay $$

Caribbean buffet featuring locally caught seafood served over the beach at Trellis Bay. Eat your fill for US$30 and settle in at a picnic table during one of the summer's legendary full-moon parties.

Scrub Island

Brandywine Estate Restaurant $$

Overlooking the water like something from a postcard, Brandywine serves elegant Mediterranean dishes with Caribbean flair. Dine on lamb tagine or grilled fish, sip fine wine, and savor the view. Romantic and refined without feeling stuffy – perfect for sunset dinners.

Red Rock $$

A laid-back favorite on Tortola's East End, Red Rock blends hearty portions with seaside ease. Think coconut shrimp, truffle fries and grilled mahi in a relaxed, open-air setting. Friendly staff, cold drinks and satisfying eats just outside Parham Town.

Souvenirs & Swag

Sunny Caribbee Spice Shop & Art Gallery

A fragrant whirlwind of spice, art and Caribbean charm. Walk in for pepper sauce, walk out with handmade prints, sea salt and a new obsession with island flavors.

Nutmeg Designs

A shop with soul. Canvas bags made from old sails, sea-salt soap and island-made decor. Nutmeg feels like shopping with purpose – and with just enough salt air to believe it.

Latitude 18°

Island-casual meets surf-town slick. From board shorts to polarized shades, this shop outfits you for both the ocean and the bar. Everything you need for a day, week or month in the sand.

Crafts Alive Market

A patchwork of color, culture and conversation. Local artisans sell handmade jewelry, batik and baskets from pastel-painted huts. Bargain with a smile. Leave with stories woven into every stitch.

Taino Boutique

Step inside for island-made goods with personality – bold earrings, breezy fabrics,

BVI Emancipation Festival

M TIMOTHY O'KEEFE/ALAMY

carved wood and a hint of folklore. It's a celebration of craft that feels thoughtful and beautiful.

 ## For Festival-Lovers

BVI Emancipation Festival

A raucous, soul-stirring celebration marking the abolition of slavery in 1834. Think sunrise street parties (J'ouvert), calypso showdowns, gospel nights, and a grand parade pulsing through Road Town. It's history, culture and revelry rolled into one unforgettable experience. Held in late July or early August.

BVI Music Festival

Cane Garden Bay transforms into a musical haven, hosting a three-day extravaganza over Memorial Day Weekend (May), featuring genres from reggae to jazz. With the ocean as your backdrop and local delicacies in hand, it's a sensory feast.

Trellis Bay Full-Moon Parties

Each full moon ignites a beachside bash with fireballs, steel drums and dancing under the stars. A monthly ritual where locals and travelers alike let loose in lunar-lit revelry. A psychedelic-friendly affair.

TORTOLA REVIEWS

26 Sailing Trip Through the
LITTLE SISTERS

STARLIGHT | SAILS | SEA STORIES

Beneath the billow of sailcloth, the BVI take on an entirely different form. Separated from resorts and unrestricted by land, its islands open up into a miniature world of sparsely populated beaches – each with its own pint-sized sea stories and legends.

🗺 How to

Getting there Sailing yachts are to these waters as a Ford Mustang is to Route 66, and renting one can be accessible with the right plan. Charters depart regularly from Road Town, Soper's Hole and Spanish Town.

When to go December to April offers the best combination of winds and weather.

Top tip Split the bill. Most yachts have room for friends and family.

Go without wi-fi Many charters offer wi-fi services, but satellite-based internet on ships can cost US$50 per day for shoddy service.

Norman Island

Snorkelers adore uninhabited Norman Island for its accessible sea caves, perfect for exploring from anchorages in its largest harbor, the Bight. Nearby, iconic beach bar **Pirates Bight** and floating bar **Willy T's** deliver rum-soaked refreshments to transient sailors.

Norman Island has no permanent residents, aside from wild goats, but it is home to a real-life pirate treasure.

In 1750 the crew of the Spanish treasure galleon *Nuestra Señora de Guadalupe* mutinied and made off with 55 chests of silver coins. The treasure made its way to Norman Island, where it was buried. In one of the few documented cases of real buried pirate treasure, the residents of Tortola – a swashbuckling group themselves – caught wind of the stash and sailed to Norman Island to uncover it for themselves.

🗺 A Chain of Many Names

Unofficially known as the Little Sisters, the cluster of small islands tracing a line south of Tortola towards Virgin Gorda are also called the Southern Islands or the Sisters. Regardless, charter captains have built a thriving industry out of overnight sails here.

Top left Willy T's **Left** Pirates Bight
Above Norman Island

Dead Chest Island

If the name of this island sounds like a fairy tale to you, you're not far from the truth. Named by English buccaneers during the golden age of piracy, this island is thought to have been the inspiration for Robert Louis Stevenson's *Treasure Island*.

It's here – on these low-slung, sparsely vegetated shores – that 15 men sat on a dead man's chest with a bottle of rum. And it's here that sailors often come to moor their lines while charter guests swim, snorkel and explore one of the Caribbean's most mysterious islands. Though nearby Norman Island is home to a historical horde of pirate treasure, the literary lore of piracy is kept alive right here on Dead Chest Island.

Peter Island

While approximately half of Peter Island is dedicated to a private yacht club, the other half remains deserted. And it's here where private sailing charters enjoy anchorages at their leisure.

⛵ How Charter Yachts Work

'The company I work with, **DreamYacht WorldWide**, has brokers that make bookings. They reserve a yacht for you online, and I think it's the best way to see the BVI. The BVI is comprised of 62 offshore islands. You can't see most of them from a resort. But you can get a lovely, 46ft yacht with premium cabins that sleeps 10 people for US$6000 a week. Then you can see a different island every day.'

Born in Antigua and Barbuda, charter captain **Alak Mansoor** has been sailing professionally for nearly 20 years. *dreamyachtcharter.com*

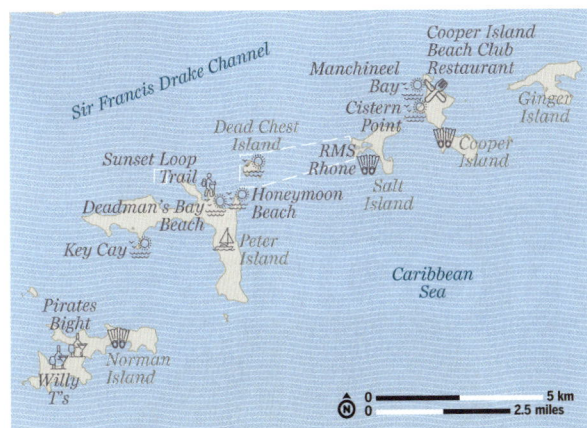

Left Peter Island **Below** Cooper Island Beach Club Restaurant

FROM LEFT: FRANK LERVIK/SHUTTERSTOCK, SCOTT SADY/TAHOELIGHT.COM/ALAMY

Hike the **Sunset Loop Trail** or sink into a hammock beneath the palms at **Deadman's Bay Beach**. Rumored to be named after marooned pirates, this mile-long, crescent-shaped beach looks like a Corona advertisement come to life. Stroll or swim over to **Honeymoon Beach**, on the east end of the bay, or pack up your mask and fins for a sail around the green, rolling hills of the island.

A short sail to the south side of Peter Island unlocks undisturbed swimming and snorkeling at tiny, seldom-visited **Key Cay**.

Cooper Island and Salt Island

Break out dive tanks for a trip to the wreck of the **RMS *Rhone***, a Royal Mail Ship that fell victim to reefs off Salt Island in 1867. If diving isn't your bag, try snorkeling off Cooper Island – join the sea turtles at **Cistern Point** or head to **Manchineel Bay**, where rays are known to gather in large numbers.

One of the most popular outer islands in the BVI, Cooper Island is a relative hub of activity. Grab dinner at the **Cooper Island Beach Club Restaurant**, which opens its doors to guests visiting from anchored yachts (reservations recommended: cooperislandbeachclub.com). Enjoy a pint, piña colada or painkiller in the bay, where tables are often set in the warm, Caribbean surf for wading visitors to enjoy.

VIRGIN GORDA

THE BATHS | HIKING | SNORKELING

RESEARCHED BY JOE SILLS

- **Trip Builder** (p148)
- **Practicalities** (p149)
- **Scramble Through the Baths** (p150)
- **Bushwack Over Gorda Peak** (p152)
- **Kayak to Prickly Pear Island** (p154)
- **Undersea Life** (p156)
- **Snorkel & Savor Savannah Bay** (p158)
- **Live the High Life at Oil Nut Bay** (p160)
- **Listings** (p162)

0 5 km
0 2.5 miles
Bushwack over jungle-encrusted volcanic topsoil at **Gorda Peak** (p152).
10 min from Spanish Town
Sample freshly grilled parrotfish in **Spanish Town** (p149).
Kayak to secluded beaches at **Prickly Pear Island** (p154).
40 min from Leverick Bay
Necker Island
Mosquito Island
Prickly Pear Island
Leverick Bay
Gorda Peak
George Dog
The Dogs
West Dog
Great Dog
Snorkel over colorful coral reefs at **Savannah Bay** (p158).
5 min from Spanish Town
Spanish Town
Caribbean Sea
Hike over the rocky shoreline of **Devil's Bay National Park** (p151).
10 min from Spanish Town
Scramble through boulder fields at natural baths at the **Baths National Park** (p150; pictured).
10 min from Spanish Town
Fallen Jerusalem

VIRGIN GORDA

Trip Builder

At first glance, this island seems packed. Ferry docks bustle with roller bags and a blend of European and American tourists. This is deceiving. Most are bound for gated resorts, but Virgin Gorda's natural wonders reward those who take the path less traveled.

Practicalities

ARRIVING

Spanish Town Ferry Terminal is the main docking point for inter-island ferries connecting Virgin Gorda to Beef Island, Tortola. Unless you're on a private charter yacht, this will be your entry point.

FIND YOUR WAY

If you're going hiking, download AllTrails. For kayaking, try the Navionics app to see bathymetric maps of the area.

MONEY

Expect to pay between US$500 and US$3000 per night at resorts and around US$200 for a midrange hotel in Spanish Town.

WHERE TO STAY

Area	Pros/Cons
Leverick Bay	Midrange marina resorts with restaurants and water-sports rentals.
Spanish Town	More budget-conscience hotels with access to the majority of the island's restaurants and services.
Little Dix Bay	Ultra-luxury resorts with stunning views and jaw-dropping amenities and price tags.

EATING & DRINKING

Virgin Gorda is home to both casual and upscale dining – cozy confines to indulge in Caribbean fare no matter your budget. At the **Island Pot Restaurant** in Spanish Town, tender, foiled parrotfish await, and **Chez Bamboo** (pictured) dishes out garden-fresh salads with an Asian-inspired twist in a bohemian beach setting.

Best presentation
Nova (p161)

Must-try barbecue
Hog Heaven (p153)

GETTING AROUND

Ferry Ferries from Spanish Town lead back to Tortola. Ferries at Gun Creek lead to resorts like Bitter End and Oil Nut Bay.

Rental car
A rental car is the best way to unlock the island's potential outside of resorts. Check out Speedy's Car Rental. It also runs a ferry and will pick you up from the docks in Spanish Town.

VIRGIN GORDA FIND YOUR FEET

DEC–APR
High season means dry, warm weather and cooling trade winds.

MAY–JUN
Shoulder season still offers good weather, though it's slightly more humid.

JUL–NOV
Low season coincides with the potential for hurricanes. Some businesses close for the season.

Scramble Through
THE BATHS

BOULDERS | CAVES | CRASHING SURF

You've seen the photo – a couple, arms locked, in a backlit sea cave, the tide rushing in around their waists as eternity unfurls around them. This is the iconic photo of the British Virgin Islands, and it's captured hundreds of times per year at the Baths National Park. Capture it yourself, or snag a fun-filled selfie with friends by scrambling through the smooth boulder field on Virgin Gorda's southwestern shores.

How to

Getting around Take a cab or drive over to Top of the Baths. Bring cash for the US$3 entry fee. The path to the beach is a short walk downhill.

When to go Aim to be the first person in the parking lot. The Baths get crowded quickly, but the first hour tends to be calm, with enough space for photography.

Top tip Bring a travel tripod and a dry bag.

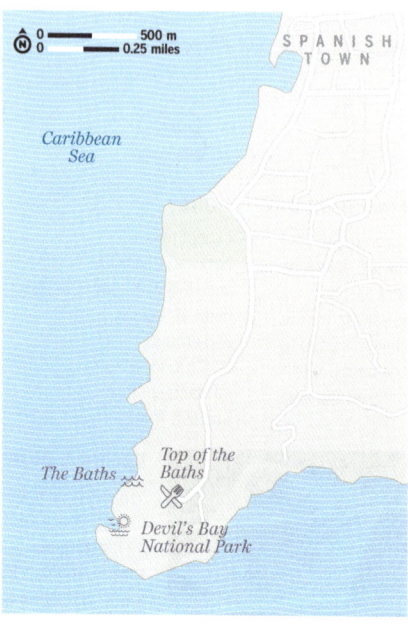

Rise with the sun and make your way to the Baths by opening time at 9am. You want to climb through these caves and feel your hands slide along the smooth, granite boulders. You want that shot of sunlight scattering into a surf-strewn turquoise cave while you bask in its glow. And so does every traveler at every resort on the island.

Prepare for your visit to this epochal national park by first ensuring you have cash for the entry fee of just US$3. The trail should be almost empty if you arrive just before opening. From the parking lot alongside **Top of the Baths**, trail signs pointing down towards the baths themselves are easy to follow.

Top Snorkeling the Baths
Bottom Signs point the way

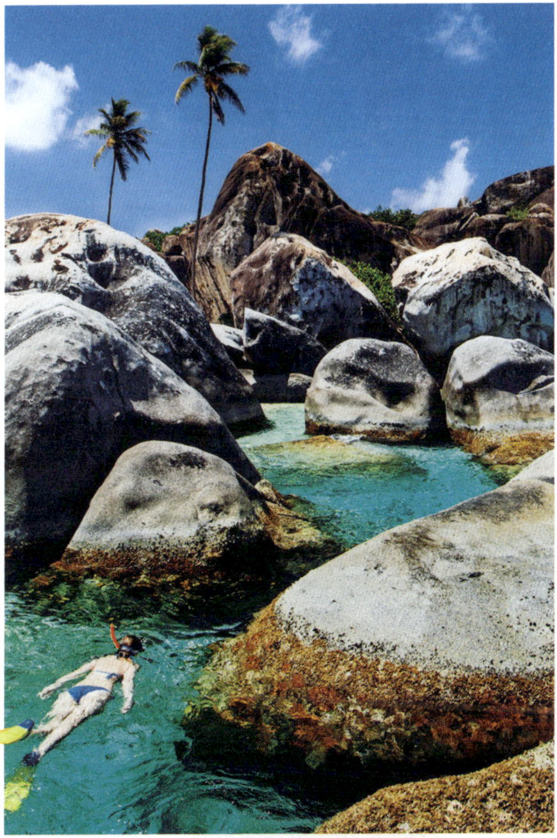

🏔️ A Fiery Start

The story of the Baths did not begin with social media. Rather, it began about 70 million years ago when molten rock started seeping up into existing rock layers before eroding. This erosion of softer, volcanic rock formed the enchanting labyrinth of secret pools and caverns that draws so many to the island today. In 1990 the government declared the area encompassing these geologic formations a national park, and their already widespread allure grew even stronger.

Hiking to the Baths involves negotiating a mostly downhill stretch of sand, roots and rocks for less than a mile. It's a piece of cake, and that's part of the draw.

As the trail meets the sea near a concession stand, an opening between the rocks opens into a pyramid-shaped cavern full of glowing morning light and foaming, aquamarine waves. A portable tripod comes in handy here. Set your timer and be mindful of the tide.

By 10am, expect to see truckloads of fellow travelers fresh out of resorts and cruise ships piling into the caverns at the Baths and the adjacent beaches of **Devil's Bay National Park**. This is your cue to make a decision: join in the party or hit the highway.

28 Bushwack Over
GORDA PEAK

SWITCHBACKS | SERPENTS | SINGLE-TRACK

Virgin Gorda may be best known for its caves and beaches, but the island is volcanic, after all. At its highest point, rustic Gorda Peak National Park provides a canopy for midday sun and a labyrinth of trails to stretch your legs on.

GIOVANNI RINALDI/SHUTTERSTOCK

🗺 How to

Getting here & around Taxis from Spanish Town cost about US$30 one way. A better approach is to rent your own vehicle in Spanish Town from an international chain or local vendor Sunnycars for about US$100.

When to go Escape the midday sun with a walk through the trees.

Top tip Download AllTrails and you'll be set with directions in the forest. The trails are rugged but short.

🐦 Wildlife on the Peak

Wildlife abounds on these sparsely used trails. Keep an eye out for whip-tailed Puerto Rican ground lizards sunning in the dirt, diminutive Virgin Gorda dwarf geckos perching on foliage, and black and yellow bananaquits flying through the branches.

04 Drive north to Nail Bay Rd where a colorful freestanding **'Virgin Gorda' sign** looks out over the north shore of the island from a commanding cliff.

Caribbean Sea

05 Claim your post-hike reward and quench your thirst at **Hog Heaven**. Soak in views of Moskito Island, Prickly Pear Island and Richard Branson's private estate on Necker Island.

Gorda Peak National Park

Gorda Peak

03 A shorter but more difficult path to the **Virgin Gorda Peak Summit** sits just north of the lookout. The rutted, rocky path climbs to the summit in about 0.2 miles.

01 There's no dedicated parking at the trailhead. Make use of **Beverly's Little Bay Lookout** for parking or find a spot on the side of North Sound Rd 2.

02 Downhill from the parking area there's a **trailhead** with a fairly gradual, 1.8-mile trail over a forested ridge, leading to a tower at the summit (pictured above).

29 Kayak to Prickly
PEAR ISLAND

KAYAKING | SEALIFE | SNORKELING

Prickly Pear Island, just north of Virgin Gorda, is a quiet escape where nature thrives. Protected as a national park, it's accessible only by boat or kayak. Visitors find untouched beaches, lively coral reefs and top-notch birding by playing Robinson Crusoe for a day.

SCOTT SADY/TAHOELIGHT.COM/ALAMY

🗺 How to

Getting around Rent a kayak at Leverick Bay. You can cheat by renting a dinghy with an outboard motor, but where's the fun in that?

When to go Seas are most calm in early summer, though the voyage is possible whenever skies are clear and storm clouds are far from shore.

Top tip Contact **Dive BVI** (*divebvi.com*) for a scouting report on sea conditions in layperson's terms before heading out.

KEVIN OKE/ALAMY

Far left top Prickly Pear Island
Far left bottom Kite surfing, Prickly Pear Island

A trio of islands sit seemingly set adrift off the northern coast of Virgin Gorda. One of them, Prickly Pear Island, holds a unique national park onshore. Prickly Pear stands as an undeveloped contrast to its polished neighbors. Accessible only by boat or kayak, this uninhabited spit of sand and sea grapes has been protected as a national park since 1988, offering visitors a rare glimpse of Virgin Gorda without pretense. Kayaks can be rented from **Blue Rush Watersports** at Leverick Bay, allowing for a scenic paddle across North Sound.

Prickly Pear's beaches are quiet, untouched stretches of sand where herons wade and crabs dart into the shelter of mangrove roots. Off the coast, a vibrant barrier reef teems with marine life – brain coral, spiny lobsters and sea turtles drifting through crystal-clear waters. Bring your snorkel. A rich, underwater world sits just offshore.

Pull your kayak ashore and take a 20-minute walk to **Vixen Point**, where a hiking trail leads to panoramic vistas of the North Sound and the island's only harbor for refreshment, the **Sandbox**. This casual beach bar serves up cold Carib beer, conch fritters and lobster salad, and sweeping views of turquoise seas below Gorda Peak.

At the Sandbox, you'll face a choice: dole out US$10 for a beach chair, or head back towards your kayak to find a comfortable log to pass the time on.

Boobies & Binoculars

This secluded haven of wildlife is ideal for bringing a long camera lens or binoculars to catch sight of some of the Caribbean's most captivating bird species. Brown boobies, greater flamingos, snowy egrets, yellow-crowned night herons and gray kingbirds are often seen in and around Prickly Pear Island.

Prickly Pear National Park spans 180 acres of the island and serves as a site for ongoing scientific research. Wander along the white sands of Vixen Point to observe shorebirds, moorhens, gulls and pintails. If you're kayaking or taking a dinghy from Virgin Gorda, be sure to pack a dry bag for the journey.

Undersea Life

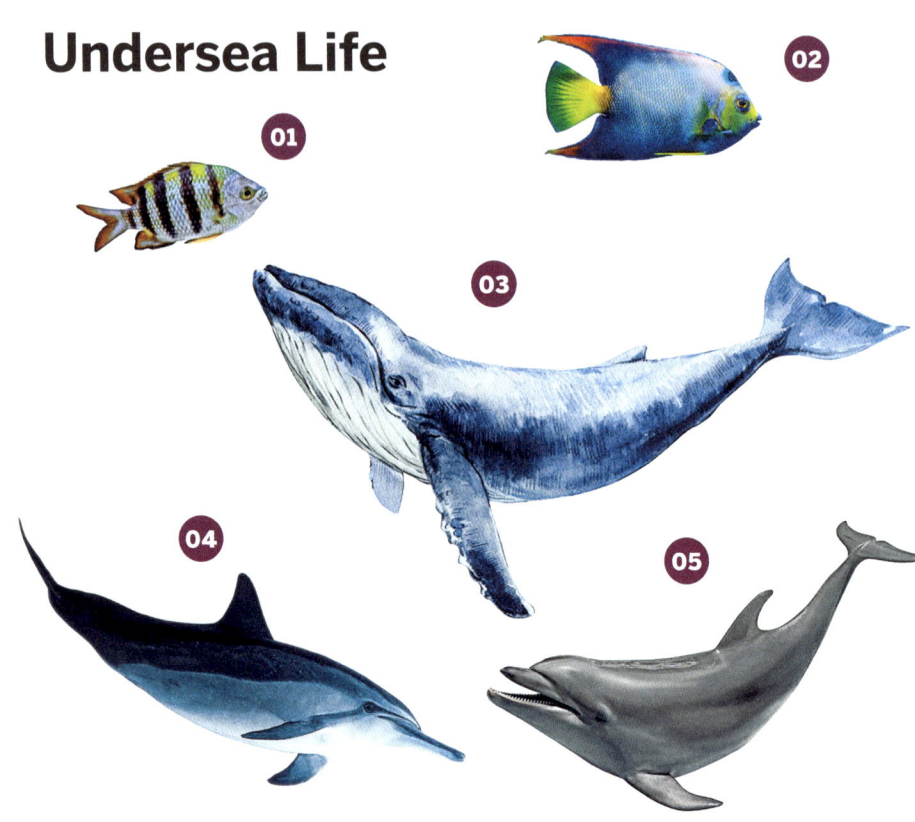

01 Sergeant Major
Often the first fish to greet snorkelers, sergeant majors are easily recognizable by their distinctive striped patterns.

02 Queen Angelfish
Look for these iconic electric blue and yellow fish around coral heads, sea whips and sea fans in spots like Savannah Bay.

03 Humpback Whale
Spot the world's sixth-largest mammal from December through April, particularly in the waters around Virgin Gorda.

04 Spinner Dolphin
Watch for these aerial acrobats when crossing the Sir Francis Drake Channel by ferry or yacht.

05 Bottlenose Dolphin
The inspiration for Flipper, bottlenose dolphins can frequently be seen at sunrise, particularly in channels between islands.

06 Caribbean Reef Shark
Rare sightings of Caribbean reef sharks happen from time to time. These impressive sharks are harmless unless provoked.

07 Stoplight Parrotfish
Sometimes seen on menus in Spanish Town, these charismatic reef fish excavate algae from coral with their teeth.

08 Barracuda
Most reefs have a guardian barracuda. These toothy predators look imposing but are generally passive towards divers and snorkelers.

09 Hawksbill Turtle
The most common sea turtle spotted around the reefs of Virgin Gorda. Look for them in Mahoe Bay and Savannah Bay.

10 Queen Conch
Large marine snails that grow up to 12 inches in length and live up to 30 years in the wild. Protected on Virgin Gorda.

30
Snorkel & Savor
SAVANNAH BAY

SNORKELING | WHITE SAND | DIVING

 Virgin Gorda beaches have a reputation for feeling...exclusive. But if you've arrived in this luxury travel playground without a pool pass and an armband, count yourself fortunate. One of Virgin Gorda's best beaches lies outside of the resort compounds – and it's completely free to access.

How to

Getting here & around Spanish Town cabs should take you here for around US$15 each way. If you've got a rental car, just slide into a parking slot at the end of the sandy trail leading from North Sound Rd to the beach.

When to go Savannah Bay is a great spot to visit year-round and at any time of day. Consider arriving in the morning if you're looking for calmer seas for snorkeling. This westward-facing beach is also great for sunset.

Top tip Pack a cooler. There are no food or drink services at Savannah Bay.

KRISTINE REED/SHUTTERSTOCK

Savannah Bay beach is one of Virgin Gorda's best-kept secrets – a long stretch of white sand wedged between shaded picnic tables and a shallow reef. Despite its beauty, the beach is often quiet, with just a handful of locals enjoying the calm, clear waters. On an island known for exclusivity, Savannah Bay feels refreshingly open and unpretentious.

A smattering of first-come, first-served pavilions hide behind shallow sand dunes and groves of sea grapes, and a nearly constant breeze keeps the tropical heat at bay.

The draw at Savannah Bay isn't just the topside scenery, though the powdery sand and turquoise water are hard to beat. This unheralded public park is home to some of the most accessible underwater fun on Virgin Gorda.

Beneath the surface lies a vibrant coral reef, easily accessible from the shore. An underwater snorkeling trail winds through this reef, where blue tangs dart

JAVIER A LOPEZ/SHUTTERSTOCK

Diving on Virgin Gorda

Distant Anegada is the epicenter of diving in the BVI, but Virgin Gorda has a healthy community of scuba divers taking advantage of nearby wrecks and reefs.

Dive BVI hosts 'dive and stay' packages in conjunction with **Guavaberry Spring Bay Homes**, a low-key collection of private cottages in Spanish Town. They operate daily two-tank dive trips that hit the highlights: the **Kodiak Queen**, Pearl Harbor survivor; **Mountain Point**, a series of underwater grottoes in Mahoe Bay; and **the Aquarium**, an isolated oasis in the seabed that draws one of the largest collections of reef fish in the BVI.

between coral heads and sea turtles frequently cruise for grassy snacks. **Dive BVI** can rent you some gear to explore this living classroom for marine life. It's a favorite spot for their instructors to wander over with snorkeling classes out of Spanish Town.

Beginners come here to learn, floating above the reef and discovering the underwater world within easy reach of beach blankets and umbrellas.

There are fewer frills here. You won't find a bartender, but Savannah Bay offers an easy, natural (and free) day of fun in the sun on Virgin Gorda.

Top left and above
Savannah Bay

31
Live the High Life at
OIL NUT BAY

LUXURY RESORT | BEACHES | DINING

Tortola is the busy. Jost Van Dyke is the rowdy. Anegada is the far-flung. And Virgin Gorda is the exclusive. The high density of luxury resorts on the island can feel exclusionary, but a travel hack can give you access to the high life for a day.

SANDRA FOYT/SHUTTERSTOCK

🗺 **How to**

Getting around A free ferry to Oil Nut Bay operates from Gun Creek every hour from 5:30am to 10:30pm with breaks at 11:30am (lunch) and 8:30pm (dinner).

When to go Year-round. Grab an early ferry and maximize your bang for your buck by departing in time for breakfast.

Top tip There is no road to Oil Nut Bay. The only access is via boat or helicopter.

SANDRA FOYT/SHUTTERSTOCK

SANDRA FOYT/SHUTTERSTOCK

Far left and left Oil Nut Bay

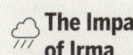

If you can afford price tags floating between US$500 and US$3000 per night, Virgin Gorda may feel like Eden-by-the-sea. And if you can't? You can easily feel left out.

Virgin Gorda is a playground for celebrities and business moguls, but at least one resort will crack a door open for the public. At Oil Nut Bay, a US$195 pass unlocks the amenities of this private world for the public for the cost of another night in a Spanish Town hotel.

Oil Nut Bay is one of Virgin Gorda's crown jewels of luxury – a secluded, 400-acre enclave designed for those seeking high-end comfort in harmony with nature. Though the property took a hit from Hurricane Irma in 2017, it has since been rebuilt and reopened with new amenities. Villas here start around US$1500 per night, each a private retreat with sleek architecture, infinity pools and panoramic ocean views.

Amenities Unlocked

Daytime amenities – the ones you can enjoy with a pass – include beach access, coastline horseback rides (US$100), spa services and beachfront massages.

Overwater restaurant **Nova** is an experience unto itself. Here, Caribbean-fusion dishes like grilled mahi-mahi with mango salsa or lobster flatbread pair with mojitos and classic dark 'n' stormy cocktails. And in late winter and early spring, humpback whales migrate off the southern shoreline. For those who seek seclusion, style and the finer things, it's an unforgettable escape that just might be worth the price tag.

The Impact of Irma

Hurricane Irma hit Virgin Gorda on September 6, 2017, causing widespread destruction. Winds over 180mph damaged 80% to 90% of buildings, including homes, resorts and public infrastructure. Power and water services were lost island-wide. The tourism-dependent economy suffered heavily, with the BVI government estimating US$3 billion in damages across the territory.

Virgin Gorda's recovery focused on rebuilding key resorts and restoring tourism, which accounts for over 50% of GDP. Many businesses reopened within two years, though some closed permanently. Oil Nut Bay reopened more than a year after the storm, but scattered remnants of shipwrecks and ruins still dot the island landscape.

Listings

BEST OF THE REST

 Lifestyles of the Rich & the Famous

Rosewood at Little Dix Bay

Founded by Laurance Rockefeller, the resort is a celebrated hideaway for celebrities and socialites. Beachfront cottages, hillside suites and villas in a mid-century modern setting.

Bitter End Yacht Club & Resort

If yacht rock was a resort. This legendary, boat-access-only enclave at the end of the North Sound (get it?) is famed for quality restaurants and an array of rentable water toys.

Branson Beach Estate

Collection of private, luxury villas on Moskito Island. Owned independently but operated by billionaire media mogul and Virgin Records founder Sir Richard Branson.

Necker Island

Balinese villas surrounded by 74 acres of forest teaming with exotic animals like lemurs, transient leatherback sea turtles and local flamingos. A James Bond hideaway for rock stars or wannabe rock stars also hosted by Sir Richard Branson. Branson himself spends much of the year here on a private estate.

 Short Day Hikes

Copper Mine National Park

Pint-sized national park featuring a short hiking trail and the ruins of an abandoned 19th-century English copper mine. Find it on the southeastern tip of Virgin Gorda and spend an hour perusing the granite outcroppings and castle-like, stone ruins.

Biras Creek Trail

An overgrown, unmaintained trail tracing from Bitter End Yacht Club to Biras Creek. Follow the stone path past the dinghy dock towards an unpaved road. There are options to continue up the hill or veer off towards the beach.

Guy's Trail

From the same dinghy dock at Bitter End Yacht Club, follow the small sign pointing to Guy's Trail. This steep trail summits a peak with panoramic views of Saba Rock and the Eustatia Sound. Return via a shortcut on the road or via Biras Creek Beach.

Mahoe Bay

Head to Mahoe Bay and stroll the shoreline for views of the Caribbean reaching towards Tortola. Swing by Mango Bay Resort for a painkiller or hike up to the Mahoe Bay View Point.

Necker Island

✨ Special Mentions

Sweet Ice Willie Taxi

You can't miss Sweet Ice Willie's silver and yellow van criss-crossing Virgin Gorda day after day. Willie *(facebook.com/sweetice willietaxi; WhatsApp +1 284 544-8073)* is part DJ, part rapper and all fun-loving cab driver.

BVI Snuba

Scuba without tanks. No certifications required. Snuba *(bvisnuba.com)* supplies guests with air via an air supply connected to the surface. 'Dive' up to 20ft deep and explore the reefs. Private tours only.

BVI E Foils

E-foil center at Deepbay Watersports *(bviefoils.com)* inside Oil Nut Bay's marine village. Learn to 'fly over water' to spot sea turtles, flying fish and stingrays. Private lessons available.

La Boheme Charters

Day sails, snorkeling charters and sunset cruises on a double-masted ketch *(virgin gordadaysail.com)*. Routes around Virgin Gorda or outer islands like Cooper Island.

Copper Mine National Park

☕ More Coffee Please

Brew at Virgin Gorda Yacht Harbor $

Handcrafted espresso drinks and pastries in a quaint, Spanish-style coffee shop near the harbor in Spanish Town. Great for a quick fix.

Top of the Baths Cafécito $

Grab an espresso, iced latte or chai after a visit to the Baths. A top-notch spot for people-watching as the crowds begin to roll in. Adjacent gift shops make for good souvenir snagging.

ANEGADA

REMOTE | REEFS | FLAMINGOS

RESEARCHED BY JOE SILLS

▶ **Trip Builder** (p166)

▶ **Practicalities** (p167)

▶ **Hover Over Horseshoe Reef** (p168)

▶ **The Ecological Reality of the BVI** (p170)

▶ **Live It Up at Lobster Fest!** (p172)

▶ **Spy Flamingos Through a Looking Glass** (p174)

▶ **The Uneasy Economics of Paradise** (p176)

▶ **Investigate Conch Island** (p178)

▶ **Listings** (p180)

Visit Anegada's most famous beach, **Cow Wreck Bay** (p169), home to a pair of infamous beach bars owned by a mother and daughter duo.
🚗 *20 min from The Settlement*

Enjoy one of the BVI's best, secluded beaches at **Loblolly Bay** (p169).
🚗 *10 min from The Settlement*

Atlantic Ocean

Red Pond

Bumber Well Pond

Pomato Point

Setting Point

○ The Settlement

Budrock Pond

Fill up on lobster and limbo into the night with Sam at **Potter's by the Sea** (p173).
🚗 *12 min from The Settlement*

Get a glimpse of Caribbean flamingos from the viewing platform at **Flamingo Pond** (p174).
🚗 *10 min from The Settlement*

Caribbean Sea

Snorkel through mounds of conch shells at **Conch Island** (p178; pictured), a popular day-trip destination.
⛴ *30 min from Setting Point*

ANEGADA
Trip Builder

▬ Home to one of the largest barrier reefs in the world, Anegada, the rogue outlier of the BVI, feels like another galaxy. Gone are mountain peaks and volcanic rocks. They've been traded for flat beaches, flamingo ponds and donkey trails.

0 ——— 2 km
0 ——— 1 miles
N

Practicalities

ARRIVING

Your likely entry and exit for Anegada is **Setting Point**. Time your visit to arrive and depart on a Monday, Wednesday or Friday – the only days ferries run here from Tortola.

FIND YOUR WAY

You're unlikely to need more than a paper map, but smartphone maps work on Anegada.

MONEY

Plan to spend US$200 to US$500 per night on lodging. Anegada's remoteness means rates can be high – especially during peak season.

WHERE TO STAY

Area	Pros/Cons
Setting Point	Reef hotels with convenient access to protected diving and snorkeling, and ferries.
Loblolly Bay	Handful of cottages and a resort on a world-renowned, white-sand beach.
Keel Point	Beach cottages and a beach club with access to pristine sands and snorkeling.

EATING & DRINKING

On Anegada, conch fritters (pictured top) are fried golden and the rum punches hit like a freight train. Beach bars like **Cow Wreck Beach Bar** (pictured bottom) and **Wonky Dog** punch above their weight with grilled lobster and spiced snapper, served with swagger and the occasional DJ.

Best party scene
Potter's by the Sea (p173)

Must-try frozen cocktails
Tipsy by Ann (p180)

GETTING AROUND

Scooter The best way to explore Anegada's nooks and crannies with flexibility.

Moke These open-air buggies are ubiquitous, and they're great for navigating bumpy roads and sandy trails. Jeep, scooter and moke rental services are available near the ferry dock at Setting Point.

Taxi Taxi drivers often loiter around the ferry terminal and near the main road. Try L&M Taxi Service for reputable rides around the island.

ANEGADA FIND YOUR FEET

NOV–APR
November's Anegada Lobster Festival kicks off peak season.

MAY–JUN
Shoulder season means fewer tourists and lower prices.

JUL–OCT
Some hotels close for renovations and some boat operators close for repairs.

Hover Over
HORSESHOE REEF

SHIPWRECKS | CORAL | REEF FISH

The fourth-largest barrier reef in the world sits just off the southern coastline of Anegada. Set in gin-clear water, Horseshoe Reef is a diving and snorkeling paradise brimming with rays, reef fish and dazzling coral.

ANEGADA EXPERIENCES

KEVIN OKE PHOTO/SHUTTERSTOCK

🗺️ **How to**

Getting here & around
There are no dive shops on Anegada, but outfitters like Dive BVI, We Be Divin' and Blue Water Divers organize trips from Tortola and Virgin Gorda.

When to go The best diving and snorkeling is from January to early June. Calmer waters prevail closer to summer months, but in general the heat picks up as the winds die down.

Snorkeling gear
Anegada Beach Club – located right on the reef at Setting Point – offers snorkeling gear rentals.

UNDER THE SEA/SHUTTERSTOCK

CARLOS VILLOCH – MAGICSEA.COM/ALAMY

Far left top Loblolly Bay Beach
Far left bottom Hawksbill turtle
Left Snorkeler, Anegada

Hundreds of shipwrecks litter the record books of Horseshoe Reef, an 18-mile-long barrier reef that has been harvesting hulls since the 1600s: HMS *Astraea*, 1808; MS *Rocus*, 1929; *The Parametta*, 1829. All told, more than 300 frigates, galleons, sailboats and steamers have collided with the fringing coral reef encircling Anegada.

From encrusted piles of ballast stones to rusting metal husks, they now form a cauldron of captivating destinations for divers. Mazes of staghorn, elkhorn, fire and brain coral form a refuge for snapper, grouper, barracuda and butterfly fish. Hawksbill and green sea turtles can be seen soaring over a lush seascape that forms one of the largest barrier reefs on the planet.

You don't have to be a certified diver to explore parts of this world, either. Horseshoe Reef doubles as a renowned snorkeling destination. Bring fins and a mask or rent a snorkeling kit at **Anegada Beach Club** for a chance to stroll right from shore into this underwater kaleidoscope.

On flat days, wreck-lovers can charter a guided trip to visit the remains of MS *Rocus*, a Greek steamship that was ferrying cow bones from Trinidad to Baltimore. Today, bones still lay strewn around the wreck, forming a kind of underwater bovine ossuary.

A word of caution: Horseshoe Reef is a ship graveyard for a reason. Strong currents make adventure here perilous even today. The reef is best explored during very calm conditions.

Where to Seek Snorkeling

Anegada is famously wild. Its waters can be sublime or terrifying depending on wind conditions. The top snorkeling spots on Anegada are all subject to the whims of the wind. But when conditions are calm, these sites are world class.

Flash of Beauty The top snorkeling spot on the island offers shallow waters and stunning varieties of coral and marine life like octopus, lobster and lemon sharks.

Cow Wreck Bay More protected than Flash of Beauty, Cow Wreck's best snorkeling is about 90m offshore.

Loblolly Bay Beach Sublime under calm seas, with great access to beach restaurants when you need a break.

The Ecological Reality of the BVI

ANEGADA SITS ON THE FRONTLINES OF CARIBBEAN CONSERVATION EFFORTS

The white sand, the rum, the reggae rolling in from beach bars. There is a real sense of paradise hovering over the BVI. But behind that postcard gloss, there's another story – a fight for survival waged quietly by environmental groups trying to preserve a delicate ecosystem in a changing world.

BCAMPBELL65/SHUTTERSTOCK

Chris Juredin co-founded one of these environmental groups. A conservationist, diver and straight-talker with a low tolerance for bureaucracy, Juredin spent the last several years listening to what the sea is trying to say. And right now, he says it's not whispering. It's screaming.

Juredin co-operates Beyond the Reef, a grassroots nonprofit founded in 2018 that collaborates with other conservationists like Unite BVI and the Cousteau family to help build artificial reefs from old boats, tag marine life, monitor whale migrations, and raise the alarm when the ocean takes another hit. On Tortola, they're helping to preserve delicate mangroves, but the group's work extends far offshore – all the way to Anegada.

'Last year, we had three tankers almost run aground on one of the largest barrier reefs in the world,' says Juredin. 'One had fishing net tangled in its prop. It was completely disabled and had to be rescued off the reef. One was disabled off of the reef, anchored for days with a tropical storm on the way. That's our prized reef. You cannot recover from one of those running around, let alone three.'

A Case for Conservation

To make the case for change, Juredin and his team log hundreds of miles on the water, conducting whale transects to document the presence of humpbacks and other cetaceans. They're using real-time GPS, hydrophones and drone-mounted collection devices that skim mucus from whale spouts. 'We can triangulate their calls, track migration routes, even build a DNA catalog,' he says. All of that, so the data can help protect migration routes from shipping lanes and protect resident species.

Left Divers obersving a turtle
Center Mangroves, Jost Van Dyke (p182)
Right Fish and coral

LOW FLITE/SHUTTERSTOCK

ALCIDES FALANGHE/SHUTTERSTOCK

But the data is only half the battle. The rest is waged in paperwork and a labyrinth of disappearing government funding. 'The Ministry of Natural Resources gets less than 5% of the budget,' Juredin says. 'We have no conservation of fisheries anymore. That's broken. We have no effective patrol boat.'

Anegada in particular sits on the edge of ecological revelation. Flat and nearly forgotten, it shoulders up to the Puerto Rico Trench – the deepest point in the Atlantic Ocean. Here, the seafloor drops from snorkeling depth to 3000ft in just over a mile. Beyond that, it plummets to over 26,000ft. 'We are just starting to find out that nobody has ever documented this,' says Juredin. 'It's too wild. The last studies were done out of Puerto Rico in the '80s and '90s, but nobody ever went north of Anegada.'

> The coral can regrow. The whales can be protected. The mangroves, if left alone, will reclaim the shoreline.

Right now, the islands are bleeding habitat. Mangroves – those tangled, briny cradles of biodiversity – have been filled in and paved over. Reefs are bleaching under heat stress. Enforcement is a ghost, and the environmental tax collected from every tourist entering the BVI? No one seems to know where it goes.

But here's the thing: there's still time. The coral can regrow. The whales can be protected. The mangroves, if left alone, will reclaim the shoreline. And groups like Beyond the Reef aren't going anywhere.

Paradise isn't permanent. But if the right people keep fighting for it – it just might endure for future generations of travelers to enjoy.

✶ Meet the Anegada Rock Iguana

Conservation on Anegada is not relegated to the seas or the saltwater ponds where flamingos roam. Spend time around the island's forested areas and you may spot a living leviathan – the Anegada rock iguana. Only around 300 individuals of this remarkable species remain in the wild.

The National Parks Trust of the Virgin Islands has implemented a headstart program on Anegada that you can visit at the **Anegada Rock Iguana Headstart Initiative**. The teams here collect hatchlings from the wild and raise them in protected enclosures until they are large enough to be less vulnerable to predators – like feral cats.

33

Live It Up at
LOBSTER FEST!

GRILLS | GARLIC | DELICACIES

CAVAN IMAGES/ALAMY

At times, Anegada feels more like a lost atoll of the Bahamas than an outpost of the BVI. It's flat, not mountainous. It's laid-back, not pretentious. And it's home to one of the most prolific lobster fisheries in the Caribbean. In November, as peak season looms around the corner, Anegada digs into that fishery to throw one of the Caribbean's most flavorful kickoff parties.

How to

Getting around Grab a scooter: the ribbons of asphalt winding around Anegada all lead to one beachside bar after another.

When to go This is a two-day affair at the end of November. Dates vary each year, but the festival is always during the last week of the month.

Top tip Take it easy, killer! The more pit stops the merrier. Start with small bites. You can always order more.

At the end of each November, Anegada ditches its quiet veneer and throws one hella-cious party for crustaceans – the **Anegada Lobster Festival**. For two glorious days, this tranquil island of reef breaks, flamingo feathers and beach bars becomes a shell-cracking, rum-soaked celebration of everything spiny, grilled and gloriously messy.

Don't bother bringing a blazer. Roll off the ferry, hop on a safari truck (or rent a scooter), and chase the smell of garlic butter down this coral island's dusty roads. More than a dozen local joints sling lobster every way imaginable – grilled, curried, jerked, and even jammed into deviled eggs. There are no plating tweezers here, just scorched grills, smoky beach shacks, and flavor that pinches your taste buds like a claw.

Between bites, there's soca music pulsing from roadside tents, barefoot dancing in the

MAURITIUS IMAGES GMBH/ALAMY

☆☆☆ Lobster Lore

Beneath the turquoise veneer of Anegada's waters lies a world ruled by the Caribbean spiny lobster, *Panulirus argus*. These armored nomads, devoid of claws, are the island's true aristocrats, navigating its coral labyrinths like crowned kings and queens.

Juvenile lobsters rely heavily on structured habitats for survival, often seeking refuge in crevices and under ledges to evade predators. Horseshoe Reef and the Anegada Channel are fisheries protected areas partially for this reason.

As they mature, spiny lobsters exhibit a fascinating behavior: forming single-file lines, they migrate across the seafloor in response to environmental cues like storm activity and changing temperatures.

sand, and painkillers poured with a heavy hand. The festival is still relatively young: it was created in the early 2010s by the local tourism board, but it's become one of the most popular events in the entire BVI since its inception.

If you're lucky, someone will hand you a cracked lobster tail still steaming from the fire and tell you their version of island history, no filter required.

At sundown, head to **Potter's by the Sea** for a final round of lobster and a limbo contest that lasts long into the night.

Top left and above Lobster fishing, Anegada

34

Spy Flamingos Through
A LOOKING GLASS

FEATHERS | FLOCKS | FUN

Your eyes aren't deceiving you. That pink flash on the horizon really is a flamingo. On Anegada, the species is making a comeback thanks to ongoing conservation efforts, and on the roadside, you can get a glimpse of that work in action.

FIANNA FLUESS/SHUTTERSTOCK

🗺 How to

Getting here Flamingo Pond is easy to spot on the road between Setting Point and The Settlement. Wildlife tours also operate boat excursions closer to Salt Pond, where the island's flamboyance of flamingos is usually clustered.

When to go On Anegada, flamingos' mating season, which features performative dancing and marching, usually occurs in late December.

Top tip Bring your own binoculars or at least a 400mm telephoto lens for optimal viewing.

MARCO BAVA/500PX/GETTY IMAGES

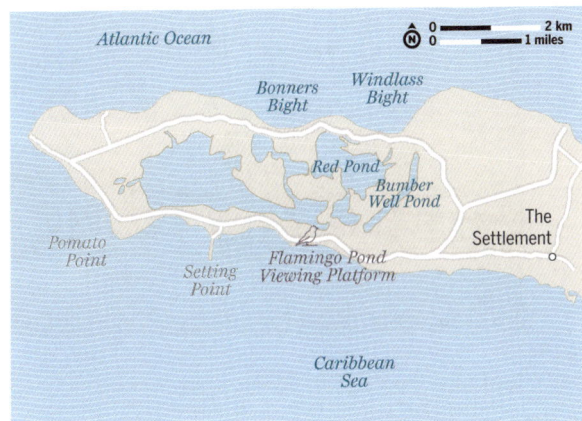

Far left top and bottom Flamingos

Midway between Setting Point and The Settlement, a peculiar wooden tower juts up from the island's sandy soil. At its pinnacle, a mounted telescope pointing inland provides a clue to this tower's purpose: it's a viewing platform. But for what? Anegada is famously flat and its best views should be out to sea.

The answer lies inside the lens. Peer inside and gain access to the secret, distant world of Anegada's Caribbean flamingo population. On most days, a flamboyance of these enormous pink birds can be spotted from the **Flamingo Pond Viewing Platform**. And any visit to Anegada is incomplete without at least a cursory glance at the ongoing drama in their avian world.

Flamingos are unique creatures, after all. They thrive in salty, briny environments like the shallow ponds of Anegada. Using sponge-like filters in their beaks, they ply the waters, scooping up samples in search of small organisms like plankton and algae. This diet tends to place flamingo colonies in hard-to-reach crannies of the Earth, like the salt lagoons of Kenya and the high mountain plains of Bolivia. On Anegada, the colonies are easily seen through the viewing glass.

Make time to pull over your Jeep, scooter or moke and take advantage of a chance to observe these charismatic pink birds in a natural habitat. Then, learn about the science behind the sights at the information kiosk.

♡ Extinction & Reintroduction

Flamingos are regaining a foothold in Anegada after being hunted to extinction in the past. As recently as the 19th century, Anegada was said to be home to thousands of roseate flamingos. These birds were prized as a source of food and fashion, their pink feathers being sold as an accessory to hats.

By the late 1960s, the last of Anegada's roseate flamingos died out. But in 1992 the Bermuda Aquarium Museum and Zoo collaborated with BVI-based conservation groups to introduce Caribbean flamingos to Anegada. The island is now home to a healthy population of the second-largest species of flamingo on Earth.

The Uneasy Economics of Paradise

BEHIND THE VENEER OF THE BVI, AN ECONOMIC CONUNDRUM IS BREWING

As tourism begins to surpass pre-pandemic levels, the British Virgin Islands are again grappling with balancing the positive and negative impacts of tourism. For travelers, knowing the basics of this tightrope might prove the difference between booking a cruise or creating your own itinerary in this pirate's paradise.

Left Visitors depart from Cyril E King Airport **Center** Charlotte Amalie Harbor (p46) **Right** Cruise ship at Crown Bay Marina (p46)

LEONARD ZHUKOVSKY/SHUTTERSTOCK

The British Virgin Islands sell a dream. It's packaged in painkillers and burned onto postcards. It's geotagged on social media and comes with a carefully curated veneer of luxury. But behind the sun-kissed marketing pitch is an economy dependent on keeping that illusion alive.

Without the next arriving plane, the next anchoring yacht, the next tourist happy to trade cash for the Caribbean fantasy, people are exposed to hardship.

In 2024 over a million visitors arrived – more than double the territory's population. That tourism surge brought in an estimated US$445 million, enough to keep bars stocked, tour boats running and families afloat. Local business owners – some generations deep into island life – depend on it. From the lady slinging fresh lobster tails in a roadside shack to the crew cleaning charter yachts before guests board, everyone has skin in the game.

But the boom is uneven. Each year, cruise ships unload hundreds of thousands of short-stay visitors who burn through Road Town like a tropical breeze – fast, forgettable, and gone by sunset. They fill taxis, crowd beaches, but rarely venture off the obvious path. Meanwhile, the same coral reefs that draw them in are bleaching under the weight of overuse, sunscreen runoff and warming seas.

Some reefs are bleaching. Some bays are getting battered by unregulated anchoring. And many locals still wonder where the US$10-per-tourist environmental levy actually goes.

Still, local businesses grind. Charter captains diversify into snorkeling tours. Beach bars double as event spaces. Artisans lean into sustainability, crafting souvenirs out of reclaimed materials like fishing nets and sea glass.

The government leans heavily on financial services too, but that world is shifting fast under global scrutiny. For the BVI, betting the future solely on offshore banking or high-volume tourism feels like chasing quicksand.

Two Road Towns Diverged in a Wood

Where will the BVI go from here?

Some hope for more accountability and stronger infrastructure. They want real support for local operators doing the work of conservation – often without pay or recognition.

> The magic of these islands might manifest in photographs and short-form videos, but it is built by the people who live here.

That means investing in enforcement boats, protecting mangroves, funding reef restoration, and giving the environmental levy some visible teeth.

The magic of these islands might manifest in photographs and short-form videos, but it is built by the people who live here. By the angler who still braves the reefs for parrotfish or lobster. By the cook who puts those ingredients together in a savory symphony of garlic herbs. By the dive instructor showing first-timers their first sea turtle, and the beach clean-up crew bringing bags of recycling off the shoreline.

Like much of the Caribbean, the British Virgin Islands are at a crossroads: double down on volume and risk losing everything that makes them magical – or invest in resilience, sustainability, and the people who call this place home.

🚢 Cruise Ships & Carbon

The world's largest cruise ship, Royal Caribbean's *Icon of the Seas,* holds more than 7000 passengers spread across 20 decks featuring 40 restaurants, bars and lounges. *Icon of the Seas* skips the BVIs, but regularly docks in St Thomas, just a short sail from Tortola.

Some of the world's least efficient ships, like the 2500-passenger *Disney Dream* and 4100-passenger *Norwegian Epic,* can emit more than 1400kg of carbon dioxide per square nautical mile, according to data from the European Union's Maritime Safety Agency. Growing awareness of this impact is steadily increasing public interest in sea travel under sail, like charter cruises in the BVI.

35 Investigate
CONCH ISLAND

SHELL MOUNDS | SNORKELING | WILDLIFE

A bizarre spectacle lies in wait just off the Anegada Coast – dunes of prickly pink pyramids reaching up from a cerulean sea. For 800 years, the pyramids have steadily grown. A tradition that began with Indigenous hunters migrated to British settlers and, eventually, to the modern inhabitants of Anegada: when a conch is harvested, its shell goes here.

FIANNA FLUESS/SHUTTERSTOCK

🗺 How to

Getting around You'll find no need for a map on Conch Island. In fact, you won't even need your phone. Navigating this miniature maze is as simple as splashing into the water and taking off.

When to go Calmer weather prevails in late spring and early summer. Early mornings generally offer calmer waters than afternoons.

Top tip Kelly's Land & Sea Tours is the go-to outfitter around these parts. It offers a half-day, joint wildlife–Conch Island tour.

FIANNA FLUESS/SHUTTERSTOCK

FIANNA FLUESS/SHUTTERSTOCK

Far left and left Conch Island

Sail to a maze of bewildering conch heaps, just offshore of Anegada. Averse to the presence of their fallen comrades, living conchs seem to migrate away from these perplexing, biodegradable garbage piles reaching 12ft into the air. Conchs can travel great distances when motivated. But with the shells clustered in a small area, rather than strewn across the entire fishing ground, a healthy population of conchs has remained around Anegada, even as the species has dissipated elsewhere.

Scientists speculate that conchs' natural aversion to dead snails stems from a survival instinct to avoid predators. Either way, while overfishing has negatively affected conch populations around other Caribbean islands, the snails near Anegada appear to be thriving.

While you can't really walk on Conch Island (ouch), you can spot an abundance of marine life in the gin-clear water surrounding the shells. Stingrays, sea turtles and nurse sharks are frequently found around the island.

Though the mounds appeared on charts as early as the 1600s, Conch Island remained a secret of local anglers, stored in their memories as a trivia question at the beach bar until recent times. These days, **Kelly's Land & Sea Tours** (*@anegada_tours_bvi*) will take you out to the piles for a few hours in the sun. A half-day tour includes sightseeing, flamingo watching, snorkeling, lobster hunting and a trip to Conch Island itself. There, you can gaze in wonder at what is truly an ancient monument to generations of seafaring people around Anegada before swimming off into the blue.

☼ What is a Conch?

More than a trumpet, conchs are living creatures. This charismatic marine snail is best known for its beautiful spiral shell and slow, deliberate movements – about a meter per minute when motivated. Native to the warm shallows of the Caribbean, conchs thrive in sandy seagrass beds where they graze on algae.

For at least 17,000 years, humans have harvested conchs for their meat and used their shells for tools, jewelry and (yes) musical instruments. Though conchs once flourished across the region, overfishing has reduced their numbers in the Caribbean. In protected or less-disturbed zones, conchs can still thrive.

Listings

BEST OF THE REST

Island Eats

Sid's Pomato Point $

Laid-back beachfront spot with award-winning lobster corn dogs and stunning sunsets. Expect a welcoming atmosphere and plenty of stories from the staff.

Pink Flamingo Restaurant and Bar $$

Snag a free shuttle from the ferry dock to find everything from barbecue ribs to grilled lobster and homemade pastries at the Pink Flamingo. Bizarrely, you can also rent an ATV here.

Lobster Trap $$

Famed for panoramic views from an open-air deck, friendly staff, and grilled lobster served steaming fresh over the sand. A go-to staple of the island. Book at least one meal here for vibes alone.

Tipsy by Ann $

Tropical cocktails, conch dishes and beachside, Caribbean cuisine dished out under a canopy in Cow Wreck Bay. Though it's one of two options in the bay, you'll be glad you stopped by for a cocktail and an appetizer – at the very least.

Big Bamboo $$$

A sprawling, open-air dining room on Loblolly Bay. Swing by Big Bamboo for an incredible seafood dinner or stop by during the day for casual conch fritters and cold beverages on your way to and from the beach.

Flash of Beauty Restaurant $$

Laid-back, casual vibes bely the iconic nature of this beach shack. Stop by for chicken roti after an afternoon of snorkeling at the identically named beach next door. Perfect for a no-frills bite in between activities or a casual evening meal.

EA's Sweet Tooth $

Homemade ice creams and comfort foods in The Settlement. Worth a pit stop to hop off of your scooter, grab a scoop and explore more of The Settlement accompanied by a sweet treat.

Educational Opportunities

Faulkner House Museum

A modest home with a revolutionary heartbeat. This museum honors Theodolph Faulkner, the fisherman who helped spark BVI's self-governance movement. Step inside for a quiet, powerful reminder of how resistance begins. A potent slice of Anegada's history lives here at this small museum – not behind glass, but in the bones of the building Faulkner left behind.

S Vanessa Faulkner Botanical Garden

Tucked behind The Settlement, this peaceful garden pays homage to Anegada's native

Faulkner House Museum

MAURITIUS IMAGES GMBH/ALAMY

plants and the island's quiet strength. Wander past flowering shrubs and tall palms, or rest beneath the sun-dappled shade. This short stop delivers a living tribute to a family's love for land, beauty and legacy.

Anegada Rock Iguana Headstart Facility

Before these rare giants roam free, they start life here. This conservation center nurtures endangered Anegada rock iguanas – prehistoric creatures with ancient island roots. Learn how locals and scientists work side-by-side, keeping extinction at bay. It's education, preservation and wild wonder rolled into one sun-drenched, lizard-loving compound.

Francis Family Farm

Saddle up and ride the edge of paradise. Francis Family Farm offers guided horseback rides along Anegada's beaches and brush trails, giving you island views from a truly unforgettable vantage. Family-run and deeply local, it's more than a trail ride that delivers a new perspective on Anegada and a salty breeze in your hair.

 Taking a Deeper Dive

We Be Divin'

Private charters cater to all skill levels, providing tailored experiences to explore Anegada's vibrant reefs and historic wrecks. Committed to marine conservation, it supports local initiatives like Beyond the Reef.

Dive BVI

Based on Virgin Gorda, Dive BVI extends its services to Anegada through rendezvous

Anegada rock iguana

diving. With over 50 years of experience, it offers comprehensive dive packages, including equipment rentals and guided tours, ensuring divers experience the best of Anegada's underwater landscapes.

Sunchaser Scuba

Operating from the Bitter End Yacht Club on Virgin Gorda, Sunchaser Scuba offers daily dive trips and PADI courses. Its valet-style service includes rendezvous diving to Anegada's sites, providing a seamless experience for divers seeking to explore the island's unique marine environments.

H2O Luxury Yachts

Specializing in luxury yacht charters, H2O offers bespoke diving experiences to Anegada's remote sites, including the *Chikuzen* and *Rocus* wrecks. Its expert guides ensure safe and memorable dives, combining comfort with adventure for those seeking exclusive underwater explorations.

ANEGADA REVIEWS

JOST VAN DYKE

PIRATES | BEACH BARS | BUBBLY POOLS

RESEARCHED BY JOE SILLS

- **Trip Builder** (p184)
- **Practicalities** (p185)
- **Swim to the Soggy Dollar** (p186)
- **Trek to the Bubbly Pool** (p188)
- **Gallivant Around Great Harbour** (p190)
- **A Song of Reefs & Rogues** (p192)
- **Jost Van Dyke Bar-Hopping** (p194)
- **Listings** (p196)

JOST VAN DYKE
Trip Builder

■ Best known for beach bars brimming with soggy dollars and sea stories, tiny Jost Van Dyke is home to some of the BVI's most enduring myths. Track down the history of Dutch privateers and the origin of the painkiller cocktail.

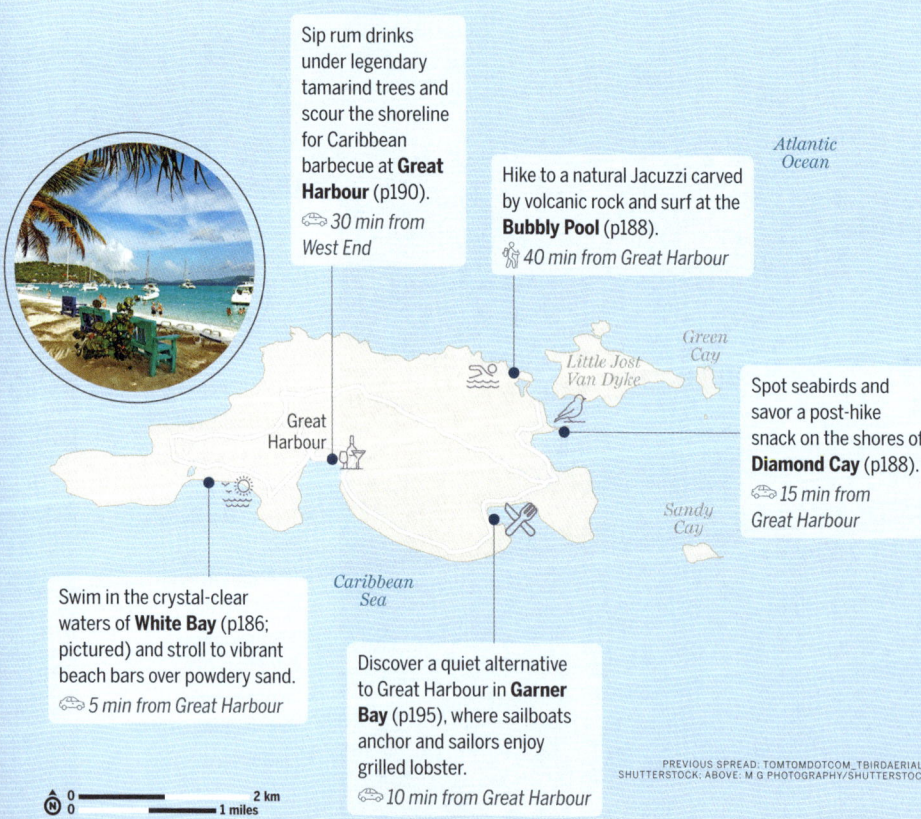

Sip rum drinks under legendary tamarind trees and scour the shoreline for Caribbean barbecue at **Great Harbour** (p190).
🚗 *30 min from West End*

Hike to a natural Jacuzzi carved by volcanic rock and surf at the **Bubbly Pool** (p188).
🚶 *40 min from Great Harbour*

Atlantic Ocean

Green Cay

Little Jost Van Dyke

Great Harbour

Spot seabirds and savor a post-hike snack on the shores of **Diamond Cay** (p188).
🚗 *15 min from Great Harbour*

Sandy Cay

Caribbean Sea

Swim in the crystal-clear waters of **White Bay** (p186; pictured) and stroll to vibrant beach bars over powdery sand.
🚗 *5 min from Great Harbour*

Discover a quiet alternative to Great Harbour in **Garner Bay** (p195), where sailboats anchor and sailors enjoy grilled lobster.
🚗 *10 min from Great Harbour*

N
0 —— 2 km
0 —— 1 miles

Practicalities

ARRIVING

Ferries from West End, Tortola, Cruz Bay (St John) and Red Hook (St Thomas) arrive and depart at **Great Harbour Ferry Docks**. Bring your passport if you're arriving from the USVI.

CONNECT

Cellular service is limited on Jost Van Dyke. Beach bars may or may not have wi-fi, but hotels are a safe bet.

MONEY

Credit cards are OK at restaurants and larger establishments, but many businesses prefer cash. There's an ATM by the Great Harbour dinghy dock.

WHERE TO STAY

Area	Pros/Cons
White Bay	A smattering of villas overlook one of the most scenic bays in the BVI. Book well in advance.
Anchor Down	The most popular method of overnighting on Jost Van Dyke is sleeping on a yacht. You'll need to arrange a private charter or bring your own.
Garner Bay	A few less-heralded vacation villas dot the peaks above Garner Bay, also known as Little Harbour.

GETTING AROUND

Open-air taxi Jost Van Dyke taxis are basically pickup trucks with bench seating. Find them at the ferry docks or beside any beach bar. They're a great way to bounce between the main areas.

ATV rental Grab an ATV rental at Salt Life Adventure Sports in White Bay.

EATING & DRINKING

The birthplace of the world-famous painkiller and a swarm of ramshackle beach bars, Jost Van Dyke's legendary party scene is littered with savory snacks and drinks. Snag sticky ribs dusted in Caribbean spice from **Corsairs** (pictured top). Devour fish tacos popping with lime and heat at **Gertrude's**.

Best lobster
Abe's by the Sea (p195)

Must-try painkiller
Soggy Dollar Bar (p186; pictured bottom)

 DEC–FEB
Peak season and perfect weather for sailing.

 MAR–MAY
Calmer winds mean the best conditions for snorkeling, diving, swimming and paddleboarding.

 JUN–AUG
Shoulder season means fewer crowds and better opportunities for sportfishing off-shore.

 SEP–NOV
Some businesses close for remodeling and charter boats go to dry dock for refitting.

36 Swim to the
SOGGY DOLLAR

PAINKILLERS | SEA STORIES | REGGAE

On the sun-drenched shores of White Bay, there's no better welcome than a swim-up bar, a rum-soaked cocktail and sand between your toes. At the Soggy Dollar Bar, tradition, saltwater and island spirit mix in every glass.

JTTUCKER/SHUTTERSTOCK

🗺 **How to**

Getting there Ferry schedules vary, but generally run from 8am to 6pm. The Soggy Dollar opens early and closes at 7pm.

When to go Stop by after a hike to the Bubbly Pool.

Cool off in White Bay and enter the bar dripping wet, as is tradition.

Top tip You're in the BVI but pounds sterling won't work here. Bring US dollars in cash or a sacrilegious credit card.

JTTUCKER/SHUTTERSTOCK

GREAT HARBOUR

Gertrude's

Hendo's Hideout

Soggy Dollar Bar

White Bay

Ivan's Stress Free Bar & Restaurant

White Bay Villas & Seaside Cottages

Caribbean Sea

N 0 ——————— 500 m
   0 ——————— 0.25 miles

Far left top and bottom The Soggy Dollar Bar

Sailors still swim like salty castaways to the shores of White Bay. Since the early 1970s, they've cannonballed from moorings – pockets full of cash – bound for the stools of the **Soggy Dollar Bar**.

Local lore says this salt-crusted bar is where the legendary Caribbean painkiller was first concocted. The omnipresent blend of pineapple, orange juice, cream of coconut and rum dusted with nutmeg is impossible to escape in the BVI. And you can take a swig of what's said to be the original recipe right here in White Bay.

Over the decades, the Soggy Dollar has expanded from the humble wooden shack where things began. And while it's possible to take a taxi to the Soggy Dollar from Great Harbour, true legends know it's best to take a swim before saddling up to the bar.

Spreading the Love

The allure of White Bay doesn't end at a single bar. The Soggy Dollar now has neighbors sharing this otherworldly slice of seaside scenery. Pour your own drink at **Gertrude's** next door, famous for its DIY-pour style. Wander barefoot to **Ivan's Stress Free Bar & Restaurant**, where Thursday nights mean a regular West Indian BBQ buffet on the beach.

Grab a plate of jerk chicken and kick your shoes off under a beach picnic table at **Hendo's Hideout**. Make a night of things by booking a room at **White Bay Villas & Seaside Cottages**.

The Legend of the Painkiller

If you like piña coladas, you'll love a painkiller. In 1970 Daphne Henderson whipped it up at a six-seat shack on Jost Van Dyke's White Bay you know as the Soggy Dollar Bar.

Henderson guarded the recipe like a secret religion. Charles Tobias, founder of Pusser's Rum, spent two years trying to pry it loose. When she wouldn't budge, he reverse-engineered it: four parts pineapple, one coconut cream, one orange juice, all riding a wave of Pusser's Rum. Trademarked in the '80s, it's now legend – smooth, tropical, and just strong enough to forget the world. Try the original recipe in White Bay.

37 Trek to the BUBBLY POOL

TIDES | FOAM | SANDY SHORES

Jost Van Dyke may be a party island at heart, but beyond the rum punches and beach bars lies one of the British Virgin Islands' most playful natural wonders. The Bubbly Pool promises adventure for those willing to chase it. Waves here crash through volcanic rock to create nature's own seaside Jacuzzi surrounded by sun, scrub and the scent of the sea.

🗺 How to

Getting here & around Rent an ATV in White Bay or grab a cab to Diamond Cay if you plan to imbibe. Tell them you're headed for the Bubbly Pool and the driver will arrange a scheduled pickup time.

When to go Early morning makes for a more pleasant hike before the heat kicks in. Late afternoon means you'll be racing to the ferry docks on the way home. High tide means a more bubbly pool.

Top tip Don't swim in the pool or climb the rocks if the surf is strong. Things can get dangerous.

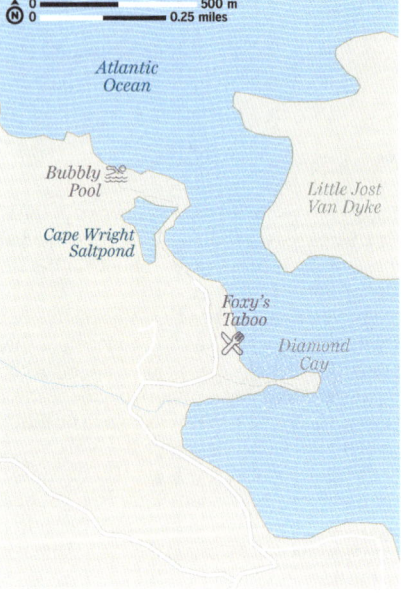

Travelers usually arrive on Jost Van Dyke with visions of lounge chairs and painkillers. But a few strong doses of the island's signature cocktail inevitably foster a thirst for adventure and a desire to trek to the Bubbly Pool. Proceed with caution, however, because accidents at the pool do happen.

Cab drivers are happy to ferry you to the island's northern coast; just make sure to arrange a return trip when you're dropped off. From Great Harbour or White Bay, a simple request for the Bubbly Pool launches a ramshackle ride that skirts the coastline to a drop-off point near **Foxy's Taboo**.

The waters of **Diamond Cay** shimmer offshore, marking the start of a short but memorable trek.

Follow the Pebbly Road

The trail winds north from here for about 20 minutes, crossing pebbly paths dotted with cacti and sun-bleached coral before climbing towards Jost Van Dyke's most-visited

JOHN TOMLIN/SHUTTERSTOCK

⚠ Fire Coral Follies

The Bubbly Pool is home to a lesser-known sea creature that can put a damper on your hike: fire coral. Fire coral isn't actually coral – it's a stinging hydrozoan, a creature sort of like a jellyfish, that packs a punch. Fire coral often appears as yellowish or brownish branching formations or encrusted sheets on rocks and reefs. Strong waves can wash your body right into it.

Even a light brush can cause burning blisters or a rash. If stung, rinse the area with salt water (not fresh water) and apply vinegar to neutralize the toxins. Foxy's Taboo keeps some on hand.

natural wonder. Tucked between cliffs, the Bubbly Pool awaits.

This tidal phenomenon forms when waves from the open sea explode over jagged rocks and cascade into a sheltered basin. On calm days, the water fizzes like a shaken soda; but on rougher days, it's a natural wave pool, delivering a frothy,

adrenaline-pumping swim that's now been documented on countless GoPros.

For those preferring to stay dry, a short scramble up the surrounding rocks reveals a panoramic view of pool and adventurers below. After an hour or so at the pool, make your way back to Foxy's Taboo where another round awaits.

Above The Bubbly Pool

38

Gallivant Around
GREAT HARBOUR

TALL SHIPS | TALL TALES | TAMARIND TREES

Tucked between green hills and turquoise water, Great Harbour is Jost Van Dyke's gritty front porch. If White Bay is a postcard-worthy snapshot of the Caribbean, Great Harbour is a hand-sketched portrait of the same. Together, the two dominant bays on Jost Van Dyke complete the picture of life in a privateer's hideout.

MAURITIUS IMAGES GMBH/ALAMY

🗺 How to

Getting here You can't get to Jost Van Dyke by ferry without transiting through Great Harbour.

When to go Jost Van Dyke is a perfect, all-day adventure packed with swimming, hiking and bar-hopping.

Need to know Most bars prefer cash but will accept credit cards in a pinch. Cab drivers prefer cards. You can also rent an ATV in White Bay and explore at your own pace.

LAURENMOISE/SHUTTERSTOCK

HEMIS/ALAMY

Far left top and bottom Great Harbour **Left** Foxy's

Tall ships make Great Harbour a regular pit stop on circum-navigations of the Virgin Islands. So, too, do sailing sloops, small-scale luxury cruise ships and hard-run fishing boats. This is the humming heart of Jost Van Dyke. It's not bustling, but Great Harbour is as busy as this tiny island gets.

Great Harbour is a working anchorage where boats tie up tight and salt-crusted sailors come ashore in search of fuel – both diesel and dark rum. It's the logistical heart of Jost Van Dyke, the first real stop after crossing the channel, and the place where island life slows to a crawl but never quite stops moving. Spend at least a half day here soaking in the vibes.

Laid-Back Livin'

This harbor has been welcoming boats longer than most bars here have had roofs. The smell of grilled fish and charcoal drifts through the tree limbs, guiding you toward the barstools at the original **Foxy's**, where the beer is cold, the jokes are sharp and a legendary owner has been holding court over what is arguably the most famous bar in the BVI for decades.

There are few curated experiences here. Just curry from a roadside stand, a stiff drink from **Ali Baba's**, and barefoot sailors basking beneath the shade of shoreline trees. Come for provisions, stay for the chaos, and try to avoid a hangover on the way out.

☀ Tamarind Trees & Foxy Who?

Many Caribbean bars serve watered-down rum over the same Jimmy Buffett soundtrack. Foxy's isn't one of those bars.

In 1968 Philicianno 'Foxy' Callwood dragged a few planks under a tamarind tree in Great Harbour and built a business that came to define Jost Van Dyke. Foxy sang calypso, told filthy jokes, poured strong drinks, and welcomed the wandering sailors who'd sail thousands of miles just to sit in his sand-floored empire. Word got out. Even Queen Elizabeth II heard about the guy running a rum bar with bare feet in the BVI. She gave him a medal for civil service.

A Song of Reefs & Rogues

LEGENDS SURROUND JOST VAN DYKE'S VERY NAME

Jost Van Dyke's namesake privateer was a real-life, historical character. More than a refugee from Spanish retribution, he was a rogue, a runner, and a colonial-era opportunist who left a lasting impact on the BVI. Today, the legacy of Joost van Dyk lingers as a tangible remnant of the golden age of piracy.

PARASOLA.NET/ALAMY

Long before the painkillers flowed and reggae spilled from beach bars on Jost Van Dyke, these waters were crawling with men who lived by the cutlass.

Jost Van Dyke is a dot – less than 4 sq miles of jagged green in the British Virgin Islands. It's small enough to miss on a map, but large enough to have once been a hide-out during the golden age of piracy.

The island's name comes from Dutch pirate or privateer Joost van Dyk, who settled on Tortola in 1615. Van Dyk operated under a letter of marque from the Dutch West India Company, which made him a legal privateer when it suited the Dutch – and a pirate when it didn't. From Jost Van Dyke and nearby Soper's Hole on Tortola, Van Dyk launched raids on Spanish ships, stole silver from the galleons of the New World, and helped turn the Virgin Islands into a hotbed of maritime chaos.

Van Dyk fortified Soper's Hole and used Tortola as a base for a settlement of Dutch, French and English sailors producing cotton, tobacco and sugar cane. Eventually, Van Dyk was named 'patron' of Tortola by the Dutch West India Company, a title that roughly translated to governor.

In 1625 Van Dyk participated in a Dutch-led attack on a Spanish treasure fleet, prompting a full Spanish assault on Tortola. Legend has it that Van Dyk fled to the island that now bears his name as a refuge.

The Spanish Assault

When the Spanish assault came in 1625, Tortola was routed. But, eventually, Van Dyk returned to the BVI, building fortified warehouses and even founding a settlement on Virgin Gorda in Little Dix Bay.

Left Little Dix Bay **Center** Jost Van Dyke welcome sign **Right** Modern skull and crossbones flag

By the mid-1600s, the Caribbean was a full-blown theater of piracy. English, Dutch, French and Spanish empires clawed at one another through sanctioned privateers, while unaffiliated pirates seized on the chaos to carve out a world of their own. The narrow channels between Jost, Tortola and Norman Island made perfect hunting grounds for anyone bold enough to stake them out.

> By the mid-1600s, the Caribbean was a full-blown theater of piracy.

Norman Island, just a short sail from Jost, is said to have inspired *Treasure Island*. Whether it's true or not hardly matters – plenty of treasure passed through here, and not all of it was ever accounted for.

The End of the Rope

As the 18th century rolled in, empires got smarter. The British cracked down. They fortified Road Town on Tortola. They started planting flags and drafting treaties. And the old breed of pirates began to vanish. Some took pardons. Some took the noose. And some, if the stories are to be believed, disappeared into the hills of Jost Van Dyke – becoming fishermen, smugglers or the forefathers of modern bartenders.

But piracy never really left these waters. In the 1800s and 1900s, Jost Van Dyke became known for rum runners and wreckers. Locals would allegedly light false signals to lure ships onto the reefs, then salvage what the sea hadn't claimed.

Today, Great Harbour and White Bay are better known for beach bars than brigands. But if you know where to look, the bones of the old world still surface. Locals speak in soft tones of smugglers' caves. And the island's very name remains a tribute to a man who walked the line between pirate and patriot.

Pirates of the Virgin Islands

Joost van Dyk might have been the resident brigand, but he was hardly the only pirate or privateer to make the Virgin Islands a regular stop. Dutch, English, French and Danish pirates all operated here.

In fact, a who's who of 17th-century pirates patrolled these waters. Black Sam Bellamy, Captain Kidd, Stede Bonnet, Tempest Rogers and Bartholomew Sharp all operated here.

Combined, the USVI and BVI encompass approximately 90 islands, islets and cays within a day's sail of each other. Many were used as staging locations to plunder Spanish treasure fleets carrying gold from the New World back to Europe.

39 Jost Van Dyke
BAR-HOPPING

LIBATIONS | LOBSTER | LEGENDS

If you're headed to Jost Van Dyke, you're almost certainly making a beeline to a beach bar. Aside from short hikes and swimming, the island's legendary bar scene is the main draw.

DENNIS FRATES/ALAMY

🗺 How to

Getting here & around You don't need a taxi to experience most of the bars on Jost Van Dyke, but cabs come in handy for quick trips to White Bay and Diamond Cay.

When to go Many bars close at sunset, especially in White Bay, but Foxy's keeps the party going late into the evening.

Open-air Taxi is a loose term. They're almost all pickup trucks. You ride in the back.

Options Abound

Painkillers get most of the love in the BVI, but a host of other popular Caribbean drinks are made at an expert level here. Don't be afraid to branch out to try a bushwacker, Bahama, mamas, Cruzan confusion, dark 'n' stormy or piña colada. For a lighter choice, Carib lager is excellent.

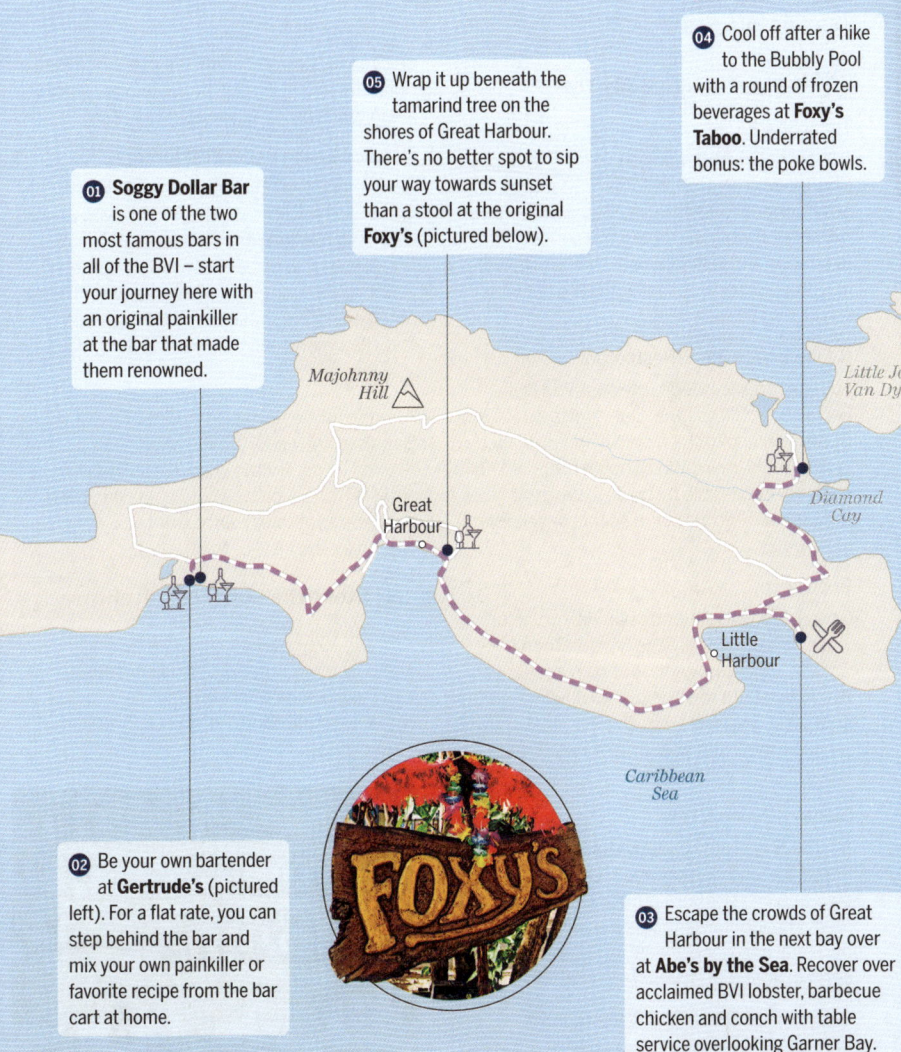

Atlantic Ocean

01 **Soggy Dollar Bar** is one of the two most famous bars in all of the BVI – start your journey here with an original painkiller at the bar that made them renowned.

05 Wrap it up beneath the tamarind tree on the shores of Great Harbour. There's no better spot to sip your way towards sunset than a stool at the original **Foxy's** (pictured below).

04 Cool off after a hike to the Bubbly Pool with a round of frozen beverages at **Foxy's Taboo**. Underrated bonus: the poke bowls.

Majohnny Hill

Little Jost Van Dyke

Diamond Cay

Great Harbour

Little Harbour

Caribbean Sea

02 Be your own bartender at **Gertrude's** (pictured left). For a flat rate, you can step behind the bar and mix your own painkiller or favorite recipe from the bar cart at home.

03 Escape the crowds of Great Harbour in the next bay over at **Abe's by the Sea**. Recover over acclaimed BVI lobster, barbecue chicken and conch with table service overlooking Garner Bay.

SCOTT SADY/TAHOELIGHT.COM/ALAMY

Listings

BEST OF THE REST

B-Side Bars to Belly Up

Tipsy Shark $

A lively beachfront spot on White Bay, Tipsy Shark offers strong cocktails and a vibrant atmosphere. Enjoy the signature Shark Bite rum punch while watching the sunset. The fish tacos and grilled lobster are local favorites. Perfect for a casual, fun hangout with music and friendly staff.

B-Line Beach Bar & Restaurant $

Located on secluded Little Jost Van Dyke, B-Line is a chill escape. Don't miss its Passion Confusion cocktail – tropical and punchy. Grilled mahi-mahi and conch fritters are solid choices. Accessible by boat, it's a great stop for a quiet afternoon or a scenic snorkel-and-sip break.

Coco Loco $

Coco Loco is a laid-back bar with colorful vibes and an ocean view. Try the Coco Loco Colada – a creamy coconut rum cocktail with a twist. Its roti and grilled chicken hit the spot after a beach swim. Expect local charm, reggae tunes, and cold drinks served with a smile.

Sidney's Peace & Love $

A Little Bay staple, Sidney's is famous for its honor bar and homemade T-shirts. Pour your own drink – try a rum punch with fresh nutmeg. The lobster dinner is a must. It's relaxed, personal and deeply local, reflecting the warm spirit of Jost Van Dyke.

Cool Breeze Sports Bar & Restaurant $

Scope out whatever soccer game happens to be on over hearty island fare. Order a cold Carib or a classic rum and Coke. Try its BBQ chicken or stewed conch. It's more of a locals' hangout, giving you a true taste of everyday life in the BVI.

Corsairs Beach Bar & Restaurant $

Corsairs delivers pirate-themed flair with great food and drinks. The Bloody Marys and espresso martinis are standouts. Breakfast is legendary, especially the lobster omelet. Great for morning-to-evening fun with friendly service and live music on some nights. A favorite among sailors and island regulars.

Ali Baba's $

A waterfront eatery next door to Foxy's. Ali Baba's is known for fresh grilled seafood and relaxed vibes. Try the snapper or BBQ ribs, and sip its version of a cold painkiller. It's a peaceful spot to eat with your toes in the sand and enjoy the view of the harbor.

Stoke the Spirit of Adventure

Jost Van Dyke Scuba

The only dive center on the island, Jost Van Dyke Scuba offers guided dives and snorkel trips around JVD's reefs from Great

Sidney's Peace & Love

Harbour. Book in advance – spots fill quickly. Highlights include dives near Little Jost and Diamond Reef. Staff are knowledgeable and safety-conscious. Gear is well maintained and modern.

Mystique Day Sails

This catamaran sailing company out of Soper's Hole offers luxury day sails around Jost and nearby cays. Swim, snorkel or just soak up the sun. Drinks and snacks provided. The crew are friendly and attentive. Ideal for couples or families wanting a mellow but active adventure on the water.

Adventure Charters BVI

Offering kayaking, stand-up paddleboard rentals and eco-tours, this group brings low-impact fun to Jost's shores. Paddle the calm waters of White Bay or try a guided coastal kayak trip. Great for wildlife-lovers – turtles and rays are common sightings. Morning tours offer calmer waters and better wildlife viewing.

Salt Life Adventure Sports

ATV rentals and tours out of White Bay. Guided tours or DIY rental options available. A great way to explore the island beyond its bars and beaches. Do drive sober.

Bunns Taxi

Take the guesswork out of getting around. Bunns offers round-trip tours of Jost Van Dyke for US$40 and one-way trips for a bargain. Schedule a cab to meet you at the docks in advance or book a private water taxi on its website *(bunnstaxi.com)*.

Paradise Jeep Rental

Another way to take the island at your own pace. Providing private vehicles for travelers since 1994. You'll most likely be in a Suzuki Jimny, and that's for the better on this tiny island.

Jost Van Dyke Scuba

Hangover Remedies

Alice's Restaurant $

Breakfast options served up over sweeping views of White Bay. Known for wood-fired pizza. Call in advance or ask the server to confirm it's on the menu today.

Rudy's Marketplace $

Beachside market in Great Harbour with basic, pod-based coffee. Upgrade it yourself with a selection of syrups and creamers.

Christine's Bakery $

Cookies, turnovers and handmade pastries. Opens early and serves until lunchtime. Worth a morning stroll or a brunch stop in Great Harbour.

Practicalities

ARRIVING

200

GETTING AROUND

202

SAFE TRAVEL

204

MONEY

205

ACCOMODATIONS

206

RESPONSIBLE TRAVEL

208

ESSENTIALS

210

Right Ferry, Virgin Gorda (p146)

EASY STEPS FROM THE AIRPORT TO THE CITY CENTER

Cyril E King Airport on St Thomas and Henry E Rohlsen Airport on St Croix service the US Virgin Islands. The only international airport serving commercial flights to the British Virgin Islands is on Beef Island, Tortola. Terrance B Lettsome International Airport operates regular flights from both the US and Europe.

AT THE AIRPORT

SIM CARDS
Not available at the airports. You can purchase physical SIMs in a major town for US$10, but this is unnecessary for most modern phones. Instead, opt for an eSIM like HolaFly or Nomad. Buy one before your trip.

CURRENCY EXCHANGE
Currency exchange kiosks are easy to spot in airport terminals, but banks in town offer better rates. US dollars are the official currency of both the USVI and BVI.

EQROY/SHUTTERSTOCK

WI-FI
Free public wi-fi is available throughout airport departure lounges.

ATMS
Look for ATMs in major cities like Charlotte Amalie, Christiansted and Road Town.

CHARGING STATIONS
Keep an eye out for scattered sockets for recharging devices, but don't expect dedicated charging stations in airports.

CUSTOMS REGULATIONS
US citizens are entitled to a US$1600 duty-free exemption if they've spent more than 48 hours in the USVI. It is unlawful to carry a firearm without a license in the USVI. Arms, ammunitions and knives are not allowed to be brought into or out of the BVI.

Medications brought into both nations should be in their original packaging and accompanied by a valid prescription.

GETTING TO THE CITY CENTER

Taxi Drivers know flight schedules and will be waiting outside of baggage claim areas. Expect to pay US$30 to US$50 for rides from airports to city centers. Negotiate the rate in advance.

Bus In the USVI, Vitran bus routes service the airports for US$2. Public buses don't service the BVI.

OLE DOR/SHUTTERSTOCK

RIDE-SHARE

Don't rely on Uber or Lyft here. The best bet is to grab a local taxi driver and store their number on WhatsApp.

TAXI

Drivers here charge more depending on how remote your destination is. These tiny islands often seem magnified by the fares.

BUS

Public transit is limited to Vitran buses in the USVI and barely existent in the BVI. In both cases safari trucks fill the gap as a de-facto public transit system and cost between US$3 and US$10 per ride.

US & BRITISH VIRGIN ISLANDS ARRIVING

OTHER POINTS OF ENTRY

In the USVI, cruise ships most often make port in Charlotte Amalie on St Thomas and occasionally in Frederiksted on St Croix. In the BVI, cruise ships always make port in Road Town.

Open-air taxis often line the roads leading to the cruise ports, waiting to ferry visitors on island tours. In the USVI, both Charlotte Amalie and Frederiksted deliver plenty of Caribbean charm within a short cab ride from the cruise terminals. In the BVI, hop on a safari bus for an island tour of Tortola. Road Town itself is more commercialized than its counterparts.

Inter-island ferries connect the USVI and BVI. Always bring a passport when changing island nations by ferry, even for a day trip. Ferry terminals are fully staffed by customs officials.

Some private charter yachts travel freely between the USVI and BVI. Check with your charter company for information on whether or not you need to clear customs when navigating between the countries. Most often, a clearance is required when entering the BVI at Great Harbour or Soper's Hole.

TRANSPORTATION TIPS TO HELP YOU GET AROUND

The best way to explore the Virgin Islands on land is by getting your own wheels. Cab fares are high. Buses and safari trucks are inconsistent. And despite their diminutive size, these islands hold nooks and crannies that beg to be discovered on your own. It's easy to grab a Jeep or scooter on all of the major islands.

SAFARI BUSES

Cheap but unreliable safari buses theoretically patrol the main islands. Finding unofficial bus stops is a cat-and-mouse game. Depending on the driver and the destination, you may or may not be picked up. Skip this hassle and rent your own car.

JEEPS AREN'T JEEPS

In the Virgin Islands, the word 'Jeep' is used like 'Coca-Cola' in the American Southeast. It's a catch-all for any kind of off-road vehicle. Most rental companies will provide you with a Suzuki Jimny or similar vehicle, though they'll call it a Jeep.

CAR RENTAL PER DAY

Compact
US$80 to US$170

'Jeep'
US$100 to US$180

Scooter
from US$70

SCOOTERS & MOKES Rental car companies – especially local rental car companies – may offer you a motorized scooter or a moke. If you're planning to scale mountain peaks, be sure the scooter is sufficiently powered for the journey. Mokes are like a Jeep but smaller. These open-air cars are a cross between a golf cart and a dune buggy. They're most prevalent on St John and Anegada, but you may see them on other main islands as well. Give a moke a go for a real-life Mario Kart experience.

FERRIES The most common way to travel between major islands is by ferry. These ferries are run by a handful of companies. Prices across the range of companies are high. Expect to pay a premium for 15- and 20-minute rides, and an extra charge (US$25) for bags.

PRIVATE TAXI BOATS As an alternative to ferries, private taxi boats can sometimes be hired. This is particularly common between the West End and Jost Van Dyke in the BVI and St John and St Thomas in the USVI. Rates are high, but might make sense for larger groups.

DRIVING ESSENTIALS

The USVI and BVI both drive under British road rules.

Drive on the left; the steering wheel is also on the left.

.08

Blood alcohol limit 0.08%.

USVI highway speed limit 55mph.

BVI highway speed limit 50mph.

ROCKY ROADS

Island roads can be rutted, bumpy and full of potholes. While main thoroughfares tend to be in decent shape, side roads can become minefields. Sometimes the pavement disappears completely.

It's worth being especially mindful when going around tight corners. Some roads feature steep inclines that are not always obvious on navigation platforms.

If in doubt, ask a local shopkeeper or restaurateur about the best way to reach your destination.

ONE-WAY STREETS Though they're not always well marked, several areas in each major settlement feature one-way streets. Smartphone maps do not always recognize this fact. Be sure to double-check the traffic flow before turning into an unfamiliar avenue. Locals may stop to berate a careless tourist.

DRIVING UNDER THE INFLUENCE

The legal BAC limit in both countries is 0.08% and penalties can include both fines and imprisonment. In practice, enforcement is sporadic and lax – especially for tourists. It's not worth pushing your luck or putting other lives in danger. Designate a driver.

US & BRITISH VIRGIN ISLANDS GETTING AROUND

KNOW YOUR CARBON FOOTPRINT A round-trip flight from London Heathrow to the Virgin Islands is estimated to emit about 2 tons of carbon dioxide per passenger. From New York, the same flight would emit just under 1 ton of carbon dioxide per passenger.

There are a number of carbon calculators online. We use Resurgence at resurgence.org/resources/carbon-calculator.

FERRY JOURNEYS

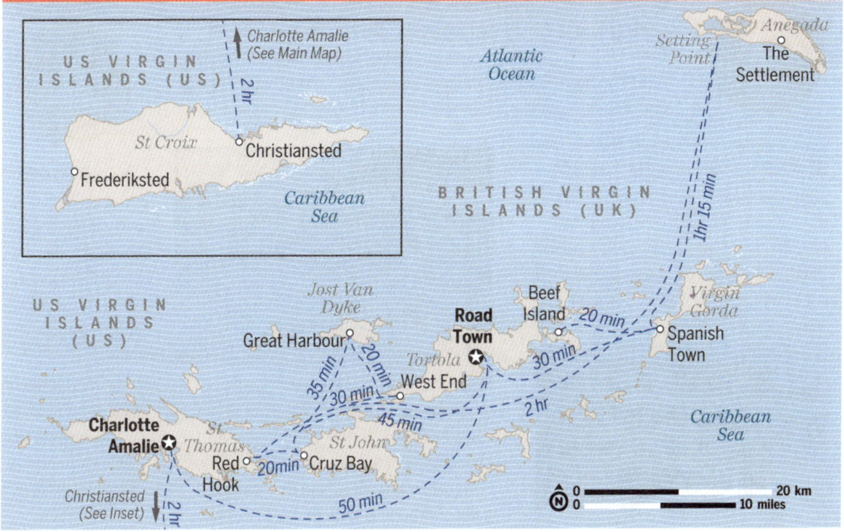

Charlotte Amalie (See Main Map)

US VIRGIN ISLANDS (US)

2 hr

St Croix — Christiansted

Frederiksted

Caribbean Sea

Atlantic Ocean

Setting Point — The Settlement

Anegada

BRITISH VIRGIN ISLANDS (UK)

1hr 15 min

US VIRGIN ISLANDS (US)

Jost Van Dyke

Great Harbour

35 min — 20 min — 30 min — West End

Road Town

Tortola

Beef Island — 20 min

Virgin Gorda

Spanish Town

30 min

45 min

2 hr

Charlotte Amalie

St Thomas

Red Hook — 20min — Cruz Bay — St John

50 min

Christiansted (See Inset) 2 hr

Caribbean Sea

0 — 20 km
0 — 10 miles

SAFE TRAVEL

Gun violence is a problem in the USVI, particularly on St Croix and St Thomas. Crime rates are low in the BVI. Road and water safety are generally the biggest safety concerns. Petty crime, like pickpocketing and bag snatching, can occur anywhere.

HURRICANES Hurricane season begins in June and intensifies towards the end of summer. The season can trail into autumn, and storms here have been known to debilitate the country. Hurricane forecasts generally give up to a week's warning – plenty of time to get out. When booking during hurricane season, ensure your travel insurance covers trip interruptions due to storms.

MARINE LIFE Waters around the Virgin Islands are full of enchanting marine life, some of which can harm you if touched. Stingrays and lionfish have venomous spines that can cause pain and serious injury. Sharks and barracudas can bite, although conflict with divers and swimmers is extremely rare.

UV RAYS The UV Index in the Virgin Islands often ranges between 7 and 11 during midday hours. Clear skies and proximity to the equator mean direct sunlight delivers especially intense UV radiation here. Prolonged exposure can lead to premature aging and skin cancers like basal cell, squamous cell and melanoma.

STINGS Scorpions, sea urchins and some species of venomous jellyfish inhabit the Virgin Islands. Scorpions love decaying wood. Sea urchins often inhabit reefs and can be found on rocks near the shoreline. Box jellyfish are sometimes seen.

MARK J CALVERT/SHUTTERSTOCK

OLE DOR/SHUTTERSTOCK

WATER SAFETY The Virgin Islands are a hot spot for snorkeling, but tidal conditions, winds and currents can prove challenging in many areas. Swim in your comfort zone. Call a local dive shop for sea conditions and recommendations.

TAP WATER
Tap water in both the BVI and USVI is considered safe to drink. Though some instances of excess copper and lead periodically pop up, tap water is treated here. Bring a water bottle and enjoy.

MOSQUITOES
Mosquitoes can carry illnesses like dengue fever, chikungunya and the Zika virus in the Virgin Islands. Use insect repellant (day and night) or wear long-sleeved shirts to help reduce exposure to mosquito-borne diseases.

QUICK TIPS TO HELP YOU MANAGE YOUR MONEY

CREDIT CARDS Credit cards are widely accepted throughout the islands. Even Jost Van Dyke's legendary Soggy Dollar Bar will take a soggy credit card if you're in a bind. However, some of the most remote beach bars are still cash-only. Taxi drivers also prefer cash, but may accept mobile payments. Be sure to ask in advance. It's a good idea to keep at least some cash on you.

CURRENCY

US dollar

HOW MUCH FOR A...

bottle of sunscreen
US$20

snorkel and mask
US$40

painkiller
US$9

BANKS & ATMS Banks are concentrated in major settlements. ATMs can be found on major islands, often hidden beside a beach bar or inside of a supermarket.

TIPPING
Tip like an American in both the USVI and BVI. A 15% to 20% tip is customary and expected, even in the BVI. Many business include a 10% to 15% service fee for tipping in their bill.

HAGGLING
Haggling is generally not a widespread practice in the Virgin Islands, especially at upscale shops. It is considered appropriate for high-ticket items (over US$500), but not on items under US$100.

PAYING THE BILL
Rental services will ask for a credit card. At restaurants, it is common to ask for the bill after your meal. Bars sometimes pay per drink.

MONEY CHANGERS
Money changers are available at banks and in major airports. ATMs also allow withdrawals from most foreign accounts as US dollars.

WHY THE DOLLAR EVERYWHERE?
The BVI officially adopted the US dollar as currency in 1959, and has doubled down on the commitment to the dollar as recently as 2019. Part of this is due to the nation's proximity to the US mainland. Another reason has to do with international businesses: around 40% of all of the world's offshore companies are formed in the BVI. Using US dollars as the official currency simplifies local transactions with the USVI and global transactions for its businesses.

WHY SO EXPENSIVE?
The Virgin Islands are generally considered an expensive travel destination. High costs for transportation, food, lodging and activities combine with government taxes and fees to increase costs at virtually every turn. The logistics of supplying islands with essentials for residents and tourists means anything not grown on an island is imported.

UNIQUE AND LOCAL WAYS TO STAY

Bedding down in the Virgin Islands can mean anything from a five-star, ultra-luxury seaside villa near a helipad to rolling gently with the waves in a sailing yacht's bunk. Though it may feel like the country caters to tech moguls and the global elite, lodging doesn't always have to break the bank. There are plenty of more budget-friendly, three-star options.

HOW MUCH FOR A...

jungle tree house on Tortola
US$150

boutique hotel in Charlotte Amalie
US$250

night on Necker Island
US$5400

SANDRA FOYT/SHUTTERSTOCK

LUXURY RESORTS

The Virgin Islands are over-flowing with luxury resorts. Some, like Lovango Cay and Necker Island, operate on private islands. Some operate from coveted coves and peaks. Others – especially on main islands, like Leverick Bay (pictured) on Virgin Gorda and Sebastian's on the Beach on Tortola – regularly offer lower price points.

Most resorts include beach access and excursion opportunities like sailing or snorkeling. A few even have access to equestrian sports and dive shops.

Rates range from around US$400 a night during peak season to US$2000-plus.

TREE HOUSES

A handful of private rental hosts have seized on their location to create miniature jungle hideaways, especially on larger islands. It's possible to rent one of these via the usual apps if you plan your trip in advance or score a last-minute opening.

ROBERT HARDING/ALAMY

HOTELS

Look for standard two- or three-star hotel rooms in major settlements. The USVI are packed with historic, boutique hotels such as Villa Santana in Charlotte Amalie. In the BVI, colorful concrete cabins like Fischer's Cove Beach Hotel in Spanish Town offer island vibes at lower rates than luxury resorts.

CHARTER YACHTS

Like resorts, charter yachts range in amenities. It's possible to book a modest sailing yacht and share the cost with friends to save some coin. It's also possible to spend tens of thousands of dollars on one. The benefit? Lazy days above pristine reefs and nights beside hidden, uninhabited islands.

Charter yachts are typically secured through brokerage websites. Think Airbnb or VRBO, but for boats. To investigate your options, try scouring sites like Moorings or DreamYacht Worldwide.

LEONARD ZHUKOVSKY/SHUTTERSTOCK

Just like vacation rentals, individual boats are not typically owned by the brokerage companies. That means make, model and quality can vary widely. Some boats are relatively rustic. Others resemble play toys for billionaires. It's essential to talk to your brokerage agent and be specific about what your needs are: how many cabins does your group need? Do you want a water maker or air-conditioning on board? Do you plan to go diving from the boat?

Chartering a yacht is the best way to see many of the smaller islands in the Virgin Islands. In some cases, this can be a travel hack, too. Groups sharing the cost of, say, a US$10,000 per week yacht might come out well ahead in comparison to spending that same time at a resort.

BOOKING

Most resorts and hotels operate independent booking sites. Charter yachts and private rentals sometimes use common platforms like the following.

Rental Escapes (*rentalescapes.com*) A luxury platform that is primarily used for private villas and private islands; for a trip without budget constraints.

Private Rentals Rental sites like Airbnb and VRBO are operational in the Virgin Islands, though listings are not as widespread in the BVI. Cut out the technocratic middlemen by going to local operators. Some – like Tortola's **SeaScape Villas** (*seascapevillasbvi.com*) – run independent booking sites.

DreamYacht Worldwide (*dreamyachtcharter.com*) A popular resource for finding charter yachts; tends to offer lower rates than competitor sites. This comes with a caveat to be particularly thorough with your booking agent in regards to which type of boat you're looking for and what kind of amenities – like showers or a water maker – you want to enjoy.

Moorings (*moorings.com*) A widespread alternative to DreamYacht that offers a different user experience and a varying array of vessel types at your disposal.

BOUTIQUE HOTELS

Boutique hotels like the **Pink Palm Hotel** (*pinkpalm-hotel.com*) and **Villa Santana** (*villasantana.com*) are viable alternatives to resorts. Many have resort-like amenities like pools and chefs, though fewer feature spa services or all-inclusive options.

RESPONSIBLE TRAVEL

Tips to leave a lighter footprint, support local and have a positive impact on local communities.

ON THE ROAD

The delicate marine ecosystems of the Virgin Islands can be strained by pressure from tourism and industry. Do your part to mitigate human impact on these islands – make small gestures with a big impact while you're enjoying the water and the shoreline.

Choose sailing charters or shared ferries over private motorboats to reduce fuel use. Bring a reusable water bottle – tap water is safe to drink. Skip single-use plastics where possible and say no to plastic straws. Use reef-safe sunscreen to protect coral when swimming or snorkeling. Stick to marked trails when hiking. Avoid taking shells or sand as souvenirs. (Beaches are made out of naturally ground bits of both, and removing them can contribute to a diminished beach.) Volunteer opportunities abound for travelers who want to take sustainable travel a step further.

EA GIVEN/SHUTTERSTOCK

GIVE BACK

Volunteer at Good Moon Farm *(goodmoonfarm.com)* This organic farm in the hills of Tortola partners with WWOOF (World Wide Opportunities on Organic Farms) to host travelers. Spend a day, week or month getting your hands dirty and learning about the flora of Tortola.

Chip in at a beach cleanup *(1beyondthereef.com)* Beyond the Reef hosts regular coastal cleanups on major islands. These cleanups coordinate hundreds of volunteers to collect waste, plastic and hundreds of feet of fishing gear along BVI shorelines.

Volunteer at Virgin Islands National Park *(friendsvinp.org)* Join a trail crew on St John. Friends of Virgin Islands National Park encourages campers to join them on Tuesdays and Thursdays for trail cleanups.

DOS & DON'TS

Do use reef-safe sunscreen to protect the already threatened coral colonies.

Don't use single-use plastics. The line between plastic and the ocean is razor thin here.

Do respect the wildlife. Flying drones above bird colonies, for instance, can frighten sea birds from their nesting grounds.

LEAVE A SMALL FOOTPRINT

Mind the reef Oils and bacteria from human skin can disrupt corals' protective mucous layers, making them vulnerable to disease. Stress from human contact can accelerate coral bleaching.

Pack it out Trail snacks are a must on hikes around the Virgin Islands. Be sure to pack out what you bring in. Wrappers break down into harmful microplastics.

Fishing line Avoid throwing fishing line overboard or leaving it on the beach. Beach cleanups regularly come across hundreds of feet of monofilament fishing line in the environment.

BCAMPBELL65/SHUTTERSTOCK

Support sea turtles with an IPA Cooper Island Beach Club raises money for sea turtle conservation through sales of its own private-label beer, Turtle IPA.

Convene with the Coral Innovation Hub The Nature Conservancy's Coral Innovation Hub on St Croix hosts regular community days with the chance to see reef restoration and coral adaptation in action.

Grab coffee at My Brother's Workshop This St Thomas charity teaches at-risk youth about hospitality through the lens of coffee and confectionery.

US & BRITISH VIRGIN ISLANDS RESPONSIBLE TRAVEL

CLIMATE CHANGE & TRAVEL

Lonely Planet urges all travelers to engage with their travel carbon footprint, which will mainly come from air travel. While there often isn't an alternative, travelers can look to minimize the number of flights they take, opt for newer aircrafts and use cleaner ground transport, such as trains.

One proposed solution – purchasing carbon offsets – unfortunately does not cancel out the impact of individual flights. While most destinations will depend on air travel for the foreseeable future, for now, pursuing ground-based travel where possible is the best course of action.

The UN carbon footprint calculator shows how flying impacts a household's emissions:

The ICAO's carbon emissions calculator allows visitors to analyze the CO_2 generated by point-to-point journeys:

RESOURCES

nature.org
nps.gov/viis
visitusvi.com
bvitourism.com
greenvi.org
business.bvichamber.org
bvi.gov.vg

ESSENTIAL NUTS-AND-BOLTS

WARM WELCOMES

Greet people with good morning, good afternoon or good evening depending on the time of day. Warm greetings are a common gesture.

WATCH YO' MOUTH

Public swearing – especially by younger people – is considered highly disrespectful. Try to maintain a courteous tone.

CONSERVATIVE DRESS

While beachwear is expected near the surf, it's customary to dress more modestly in town. Bring a cover-up for restaurants and flip-flops to cover bare feet indoors.

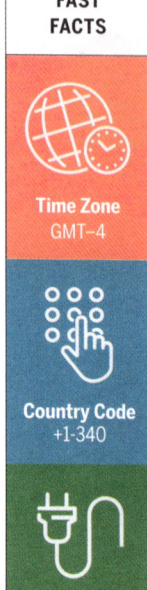

FAST FACTS

Time Zone
GMT–4

Country Code
+1-340

Electricity
110V/60Hz

GOOD TO KNOW

US citizens don't need a passport to visit the USVI, but will need a 'Real ID.'

Some nationalities must apply for an electronic travel visa (ESTA) via the US State Department to visit the USVI.

Citizens of the US, Canada, the UK and European Union can visit the BVI without a visa for up to 30 days.

Dial 911 in case of emergency.

Dial 311 for non-emergency incidents.

ACCESSIBLE TRAVEL

Accessibility in the Virgin Islands is historically challenging, but improving. Several local operators offer excursions for people with additional physical requirements.

Accessible Caribbean Vacations (*accessiblecaribbeanvacations.com*) offers excursions to Tortola that incorporate botanical gardens, historic sites and more.

Accessible beach access can be tricky. Virgin Islands National Park has accessible features. Try Trellis Bay, Savannah Bay and Cane Garden Bay for flatter beaches with easier access for scooters and wheelchairs.

Accessible dining can also be challenging. Cruz Bay, Beef Island, Frederiksted and Christiansted feature more accessible businesses than other areas.

Tropical weather can affect terrain – wet paths and sand may be more difficult to navigate, so consider visiting during the dry season (December–April).

Ferries are particularly challenging. Call in advance to make sure interisland ferries have accessibility ramps. Some boats might; others may not.

Resorts are a good option for accessible travel. Many newer resorts were built with accessibility in mind.

PATIENCE...
Island-time mentality rules: the world on the islands does not move at the speed of London or New York.

PRIVATE BEACHES
All beaches in the USVI are technically public. In the BVI, some sections may be private.

PHOTOS
It's considered courteous to introduce yourself and ask before taking photographs of people at work or play.

FAMILY TRAVEL
Book early Especially during high season (December–April), popular family spots book up quickly.

Car seats Bring your own or arrange with rental-car companies in advance. Availability can be limited.

Look for family beach resorts These differ from romantic, adult-focused getaways. Virgin Gorda and St John are better options for family travel, as both feature family-friendly resorts and natural areas with room to spread out.

FERRY BAGGAGE
Pack sparingly to save on transport fees. Ferries often charge US$25 per bag for transport. That's in addition to fees upwards of US$70 for a one-way ride. Ferry companies here know they are an unavoidable service and charge as such.

BETWEEN THE USVI & BVI
It's possible to take a ferry from the BVI to the USVI. This transit always requires a valid passport. Ferry terminals feature fully operational customs and immigration facilities, where bags will be checked and passports stamped. Be especially mindful of snacks like fruit carried between islands.

LGBTIQ+ TRAVELERS
Outright discrimination isn't common, and the USVI are generally a safe and welcoming place for LGBTIQ+ travelers. St Thomas has had a thriving LGBTIQ+ scene since the 1960s. The BVI remain more uptight, though Cooper Island has a reputation for open arms.

Public displays of affection are more tolerated in the USVI than the BVI. Though you're unlikely to face open conflict, the BVI can be a religious and conservative place.

Transgender travelers have occasionally reported harassment from local business owners in the BVI, particularly on Jost Van Dyke.

US & BRITISH VIRGIN ISLANDS ESSENTIALS

Index

8 Tough Miles 21
99 Steps 47

A

accessible travel 210
accommodations 206-7
activities 16-23, *see also individual activities*
air travel 40, 116, 200-1
Anegada 164-81, **30-1**, **166**
    accommodations 167
    drinking 167
    food 167, 172-3, 180
    money 167
    navigation 167
    planning 30-1, 166
    travel seasons 167
    travel to & within 167
Anegada Lobster Festival 19, 172-3
Anegada rock iguanas 171, 181
animals 73, 74-5, 110, 136-7, 152, 156-7, *see also individual animals*
Annaberg Plantation 77
Annaly Bay Tide Pools 106-7
aquanauts 83
Arawak people 131
architecture 92-3
area codes 210
art galleries, *see* museums & galleries
arts 55, 58-9, 63, 68

000 Map pages

B

ATMs 205
ATVs 185, 197

bananaquits 74
barracudas 157
Baths, the 150-1, **150**
beaches 6-7
    Brewers Bay 128-9, **129**
    Buck Island 99-100
    Cane Bay 105
    Cane Garden Bay 135
    Cinnamon Bay 72
    Coki Beach 50
    Coral Bay 82-3
    Cow Wreck Bay 169
    Cowboy Beach 109
    Flash of Beauty 169
    Guana Island 140
    Honeymoon Beach 72
    Hull Bay 51
    Josiah's Bay 126-7
    Lindquist Beach 49-50
    Little Sisters 142-5
    Loblolly Bay Beach 169
    Lovango Cay 84-5
    Magens Bay 49
    North Shore (St Croix) 104
    North Shore (St John) 80-1
    North Shore (Tortola) 134-5, **135**
    Oil Nut Bay 160-1
    Prickly Pear Island 154-5
    Protestant Cay 102
    Sapphire Beach 50-1
    Savannah Bay 158-9
    Secret Harbor Beach 51
    Shoy Beach 112
    Smuggler's Cove 128-9, **129**
    St John 80-1
    St Thomas 48-51, **51**
    Trunk Bay 111
    Turtle Beach 99-100
Beef Island Lagoon 136-7
Beyond the Reef 170-1
Bio Bay 105
birdwatching 70-3, 112, 133, 155, 174-5, *see also individual birds*
Bitter End Yacht Club & Resort 162
boat travel 32-3, 40, 87, 116, 201, 202, *see also* charter yachts, ferry travel
books 36
bottlenose dolphins 156
boutique hotels 207
Branson Beach Estate 162
breweries 47
    Brew STX 95
    Frenchtown Brewing 62
    Leatherback Brewing Company 95
    St John Brewers 69
British Virgin Islands 114-97, *see also individual islands*
    accommodations 117
    drinking 117
    food 117
    internet access 117
    money 117
    safety 117

travel seasons 116
travel to & within 116
brown boobies 74, 155
Bubbly Pool 188-9, **188**
Buck Island Reef National Monument 98-101
budget 149, 167, 205
bus travel 40, 45, 67, 71, 91, 201, 202
BVI Emancipation Festival 17, 141
BVI Fungi Festival 19
BVI Music Festival 141
BVI Snuba 163
BVI Spring Regatta 124-5

C

Caledonia Rainforest 107
camping 72, 113
canoes 130-1, 138-9
Captain Morgan Rum Distillery 95
car rental 149, 197, 202
car travel 35, 67, 91, 116, 121, 149, 203
Caribbean reef sharks 157
Carnival 16, 23, 54-5, 111
cell phones 34, 200
Charlotte Amalie 46-7, 55, 62, **47**
charter yachts 142-5, 163, 181, 207
children, travel with 72, 211
Christiansted 92-5, **93**
Christiansted National Historic Site 93
Christmas Cove 63
churches 62
climate 16-23
Columbus, Christopher 104-5, 131
Conch Island 178-9
conchs 15, 19, 179

conservation 170-1
Cooper Island 145
Cooper Island Beach Club Restaurant 145
Coral Bay 82-3, **82**
costs 149, 167, 205
crabs 74
credit cards 205
Crucian Christmas Festival 20, 54-5
cruise ships 40, 46, 122, 177, 201
Cruz Bay 68-9, **69**
culture 79
currency 34, 205
customs regulations 200

D

Dead Chest Island 144
death apples 71
deep-sea fishing 104
Diamond Cay 188-9, 194-5
distilleries
  13 Wimmelskafts Slave House 61
  Callwood Rum Distillery 135
  Captain Morgan Rum Distillery 95
  Cruzan Rum Distillery 95
  Sion Farm Distillery 95
diving 10-11, 87, see also snorkeling
  Anegada 168-9, 181
  Buck Island Reef Underwater Trail 100
  Horseshoe Reef 168-9
  Jost Van Dyke 196-7
  Little Sisters 145
  St Croix 100-1, 105
  St John 87
  St Thomas 51
  Virgin Gorda 159

dolphins 156
donkeys 73, 74
drinking 14, see also breweries, distilleries, individual locations
driving tours, see also car travel
  East End 102-3, **103**
  Gorda Peak 152-3, **153**
  North Shore (St Croix) 104-5, **105**

E

East End 102-3, **103**
e-foiling 163
electricity 210
emergencies 210
environmental issues 110-11, 170-1
Estate Mount Washington Plantation 112
etiquette 35, 210
events, see festivals & events

F

family travel 72, 211
ferry travel 40, 116, 202, 203, 211
  Jost Van Dyke 185
  St Croix 91
  St John 67
  St Thomas 45
  Tortola 121
  Virgin Gorda 149
festivals & events 16-23, 54-5, 124-5, 141, 172-3, see also individual festivals
films 37
fire coral 189
fishing 104
Flamingo Pond Viewing Platform 174-5, **175**
flamingos 74, 155, 174-5

floating restaurant 63
food 15, *see also individual locations*
forests 12-13
forts
  Fort Burt Hotel 123
  Fort Christian 47
  Fort Christiansvaern 93, 96-7
  Fort Frederik 108
  Fort George 123
  Fort Segarra 52, 53
Foxy's 20, 191, 195
Foxy's Taboo 188-9, 195
Frederick Evangelical Lutheran Church 62
Frederiksted 108-9, 111, **108**
Frenchtown 62
full-moon parties 14, 16, 141

G

galleries, *see* museums & galleries
gardens, *see* parks & gardens
glamping 113
Gli Gli 138-9
Goat Mountain 103
Gorda Peak 152-3, **153**
Great Camanoe 140
Great Harbour 190-1
Great Thatch Island 140
greater bulldog bats 75
green turtles 102
Guana Island 140

H

haggling 205
Hamilton, Alexander 96-7
hawksbill turtles 102, 157

hiking
  Coral Bay 82-3
  Gorda Peak 152-3
  Peter Island 145
  Reef Bay Trail 76-7
  Sage Mountain 132-3
  St Croix 99, 112
  St Thomas 56-7
  Virgin Gorda 162
  Virgin Islands National Park 70-3, 76-7
history 8-9
  Annaberg Plantation 77
  Christiansted 93
  Estate Mount Washington Plantation 112
  Frederiksted 108-9
  Hamilton, Alexander 96-7
  maritime history 130-1, 138-9
  St Croix 96-7
  St John 87
  St Thomas 62
  US Virgin Islands 78-9
  van Dyk, Joost 192-3
horseriding 87, 109, 112, 181
Horseshoe Reef 168-9
hotels 206
humpback whales 156, 161
Hurricane Irma 127, 161
hurricanes 136, 204

I

iguanas 75, 171, 181
internet access 41, 117, 200
internet resources 37
itineraries 24-33, *see also individual regions*

J

Jack and Isaac Bay Preserve 102
Jeep rentals 197, 202

Josiah's Bay 126-7
Jost Van Dyke 182-97, **26-7**, **184**
  accommodations 185
  drinking 185, 186-7, 194-5, 196
  food 185, 197
  itineraries 194-5, **195**
  money 185
  navigation 185
  planning 26-7, 184
  travel seasons 185
  travel to & within 185

K

Kalinago people 130-1, 138-9
kayaking
  Jost Van Dyke 197
  St Croix 104, 112
  St John 81, 87
  St Thomas 49, 57
  Virgin Gorda 154-5

L

leatherback sea turtles 109, 162
LGBTIQ+ travelers 211
literature 36
Little Camanoe 140
Little Sisters 28-9, 142-5, **145**
Little Thatch 140
lobsters 172-3
Lovango Cay 84-5

M

magazines 37
maritime history 130-1, 138-9
mobile phones 34, 200
mokes 167, 202
money 205
money changers 205
mongooses 75
mosquitoes 204
Mount Healthy Windmill 129
Mountain Top 111

000 Map pages

museums & galleries
  13 Wimmelskafts Slave House 61
  81C 55
  AH Riise 63
  Bajo El Sol 68
  Caribbean Museum Center for the Arts 108-9
  Creative Native 55
  Estate Whim Museum 97
  Faulkner House Museum 180
  Mango Tango 63
  Many Hands Gallery 112
  Mystic By the Sea 55
  North Shore Shell Museum & Restaurant 135
  St Croix Leap 107
  Tillett Gardens 63
  Yacht Haven Grande 63
music 36, 54-5, 141, see also festivals & events

N
Nanny Cay 124-5
national parks 110, 208, see also parks & gardens
  Baths National Park 150-1
  Buck Island Reef National Monument 98-101
  Copper Mine National Park 162
  Devil's Bay National Park 151
  Gorda Peak National Park 152-3
  Prickly Pear National Park 154-5
  Sage Mountain National Park 132-3
  Virgin Islands National Park 70-3, 76-7, 80-1, 208, **73**
Necker Island 162

Nigel's Boom Boom Beach Bar 129
nightlife, see drinking
Norman Island 143
North Shore (St Croix) 104-5, **105**
North Shore (St John) 80-1
North Shore (Tortola) 134-5, **135**

O
Oil Nut Bay 160-1
Old Year's Night 20
open-container laws 34

P
paddleboard yoga 87
painkiller cocktails 187
Paradise Point Skyride 63
parks & gardens, see also national parks
  Emancipation Garden 62
  S Vanessa Faulkner Botanical Garden 180
  St George Village Botanical Garden 112
Peace Hill 87
Peter Island 144-5
petroglyphs 77
pirates 78, 143, 192-3
planning, see also individual locations
  accommodations 206-7
  basics 210-11
  budget 149, 167, 205
  climate 16-23
  family travel 72, 211
  internet resources 37
  itineraries 24-33
  travel to/from the Virgin Islands 200-1

travel within the Virgin Islands 202-3, **203**
Point Udall 102-3, **103**
pottery 59, 87
Prickly Pear Island 154-5, **155**
private islands 84-5
privateers 78, 192-3
Protestant Cay 112
Pusser's Pub 123

Q
queen angelfish 156
queen conchs 157

R
Red Hook 60-1
Reef Bay Trail 76-7
reef-safe sunscreen 35, 49
resorts 206
responsible travel 208-9
road rules 35
Road Town 122-3, **123**
Rosewood at Little Dix Bay 162
rum 58, 61, 95, 135

S
safe travel 204
Sage Mountain 132-3
sailing 32-3, 207
  BVI Spring Regatta 124-5
  Christiansted 93
  history 130-1, 138-9
  Jost Van Dyke 197
  Little Sisters 142-5
  St Croix 93
  St John 87
  Virgin Gorda 163
sales tax 34
Salt Island 145

Salt River Bay National Historic Park 105
Salt River Estuary 105
Sandy Point National Wildlife Refuge 109
Savannah Bay 158-9
scooters 167, 202
Scrub Island 140
sea animals 156-7, *see also individual animals*
sergeant majors 156
sharks 136-7, 157
shopping, *see individual locations*
SIM cards 200
snorkeling 10-11, 204
  Anegada 169
  Buck Island Reef Underwater Trail 100
  Conch Island 178-9
  Coral Bay 82-3
  Horseshoe Reef 168-9
  Jost Van Dyke 196-7
  Prickly Pear Island 155
  Savannah Bay 158-9
  St Croix 100-1, 112
  St John 81, 85, 87
  St Thomas 50-1, 57
  Tortola 140
social media 37
Soggy Dollar Bar 186-7, 195
souvenirs 58-9
spinner dolphins 156
St Croix 88-113, **24-5**, **90**
  accommodations 91
  drinking 91, 94-5, 113

food 91, 94-5, 113
  itineraries 102-3, 104-5, **103**, **105**
  money 91
  navigation 91
  planning 24-5, 90
  shopping 112
  travel seasons 91
  travel to & within 91
St Croix ground lizards 75
St John 64-87, **26-7**, **66**
  accommodations 67
  drinking 67, 86
  food 67, 86
  itineraries 68-9, **69**
  money 67
  navigation 67
  planning 26-7, 66
  travel seasons 67
  travel to & within 67
St John Arts Festival 21
St John Carnival 54-5
St Thomas 42-63, **24-5**, **44**
  accommodations 45
  drinking 45, 61
  food 45, 62-3
  itineraries 46-7, **47**
  money 45
  navigation 45
  planning 24-5, 44
  travel seasons 45
  travel to & within 45
St Thomas Carnival 54-5
stand-up paddleboarding 81, 136-7
stoplight parrotfish 157
STXPride 16
sunscreen 35, 49

surfing
  St Thomas 51
  Tortola 126-7, 135
Sweet Ice Willie Taxi 163

T
Taíno people 77, 78, 130-1, 141
tap water 204
Taste of St Croix 22
taxi boats 202
taxis 40, 116, 163, 167, 185, 201
time 210
tipping 34, 205
Tortola 118-41, **28-9**, **120**
  accommodations 121
  drinking 121
  food 121, 123, 140-1
  money 121
  navigation 121
  planning 28-9, 120
  shopping 141
  travel seasons 121
  travel to & within 121
tourism 176-7
tours
  Anegada 179
  Conch Island 179
  Jost Van Dyke 197
  St Croix 95, 97, 104
  Tortola 136
travel seasons 16-23, *see also individual locations*
travel to/from the Virgin Islands 200-1
travel within the Virgin Islands 202-3, **203**, *see also individual locations*
tree houses 206

trekking, see hiking
Trellis Bay Full-Moon Parties 141

U

US dollar 205
US Virgin Islands 38-113, see
  also individual islands
  accommodations 41
  drinking 41
  food 41
  internet access 41
  money 41
  safety 41
  travel seasons 40
  travel to & within 40

V

van Dyk, Joost 192-3
vegetarian travelers 41, 113
Very Long Baseline Array
  Telescope 103

Virgin Gorda 146-63, **30-1**, **148**
  accommodations 149, 162
  drinking 149
  food 149, 163
  itineraries 152-3, **153**
  money 149
  navigation 149
  planning 30-1, 148
  travel seasons 149
  travel to & within 149
Virgin Gorda Easter Festival 23
Virgin Islands coquis 75
Virgin Islands dwarf sphaeros 74
Virgin Islands National Park
  70-3, 76-7, 80-1, 208, **73**
Virgin Islands tree boas 75
volunteering 208

W

walking tours, see also hiking
  Charlotte Amalie 46-7, **47**

Cruz Bay 68-9, **69**
  Jost Van Dyke 194-5, **195**
water 204
Water Island 52-3, **52**
Waterlemon Cay 82
weather 16-23
websites 37
whales 170-1
White Bay 186-7, 194-5, **187**
wi-fi 41, 117, 200
wildlife 73, 74-5, 110, 136-7,
  152, 156-7, see also individual
  animals

Y

yachts 124-5, see also charter
  yachts
yoga 63, 87

Z

ziplining 63

'The first time I crested over a hill and saw the North Shore of St John (pictured left) I was absolutely hooked.'

MARK JOHANSON

'On Jost Van Dyke, I walked from Foxy's Taboo to Great Harbour after missing a taxi from The Bubbly Pool.'

JOE SILLS

'I took a seaplane to St Croix to dive the Wall, and saw my first seahorse.'

MARK JOHANSON

'That time I woke up at dawn to be the first one at the Baths in Virgin Gorda (pictured right) was totally worth it.'

JOE SILLS

THIS BOOK

Destination Editor
James Smart

Production Editor
Hannah Cartmel

Cartographer
Anthony Phelan

Image Editor
Megan Cassidy

Coordinating Editor
Andrea Dobbin

Assisting Editors
Janet Austin

Cover Researcher
Giada de Agostinis

Thanks
Alex Howard, Alicia

Johnson, Kat Rowan, Vicky Smith, Saralinda Turner